How
to
Turn
Your
MBA
Into
a
CEO

Robert W. Lear
with
Elisabetta di Cagno

Collier Books
Macmillan Publishing Company
New York
Collier Macmillan Publishers
London

How to Turn Your MBA Into a CEO

Macmillan Publishing Company
866 Third Avenue, New York, N.Y. 10022
Collier Macmillan Canada, Inc.

Library of Congress Cataloging-in-Publication Data
Lear, Robert W.
    How to turn your MBA into a CEO.
    Includes index.
    1. Master of business administration degree—
United States. 2. Executives—Vocational guidance—
United States. I. di Cagno, Elisabetta. II. Title.
HF1131.L39   1987   650'.07'1173   86-26893

ISBN 0-02-034070-2 (pbk.)

Macmillan books are available at special discounts
for bulk purchases for sales promotions, premiums,
fund-raising, or educational use.
For details, contact:

Special Sales Director
Macmillan Publishing Company
866 Third Avenue
New York, N.Y. 10022

10 9 8 7 6 5 4 3 2 1

Designed by Jack Meserole

Printed in the United States of America

How to Turn Your MBA Into a CEO is also available in a
hardcover edition from Macmillan Publishing Company.

To my wife, Dorothy S. Lear.

—ROBERT W. LEAR

I dedicate my efforts to all the students whose lives will be clarified and enhanced by Bob Lear's words. And to my mother.

—ELISABETTA DI CAGNO

Career Strategy

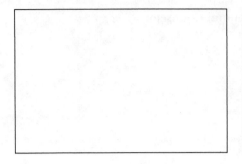

CONTENTS

Interviewing

Evaluating Jobs

FOREWORD

As editor of *Chief Executive* magazine, I have met and interviewed countless chairmen and presidents of leading corporations and institutions from around the world. During my conversations with these accomplished leaders, I try to find what it was in their personal background, education, or early business training that contributed markedly to their successful careers.

One of the most interesting men I have come across is Robert W. Lear, who, at the time we met, had just taken early retirement as chairman and chief executive officer of F & M Schaefer Corporation in New York City to become Executive-in-Residence at Columbia Business School. When I asked him to write about his experiences for *Chief Executive*, he responded with "How to Retire Without Quitting Work," which turned out to be one of the best-read articles the magazine has ever published.

Shortly thereafter I asked him to write a regular column for us, entitled "Speaking Out." I wanted him to do just that—speak out on the critical issues facing CEOs in the management of their businesses and relationships with their boards of directors. His first column, which ran in *CE*'s Winter 1979 issue, was headed, "What the Outside Director Expects from the Chief Executive." It created a small furor, since at that time CEOs had the reputation of treating directors like mushrooms—keep them in the dark and throw a lot of fertilizer on them. Yet Robert Beck, chairman and chief executive of Prudential Insurance, wrote in praise of Lear's precepts, calling them "timely" and worth implementing.

Robert Lear has written for every issue we have published since, covering subjects as diverse as executive compensation, CEO succession, greenmail, and the status of today's MBAs as chief executives in the year 2006.

Which brings me to the point. Bob (almost no one calls him Mr. Lear, including his students) is now finishing his tenth year at Columbia, while simultaneously serving as an outside director for a dozen top corporations. He has been able to balance the intellectual exposure at the school with the dynamic events that take place in the boardroom. And he is one of those rare executives who can write and speak effectively.

Lear was instrumental in organizing a series of advisory boards that brought several hundred business executives on campus to meet with MBA students and faculty. He's an excellent teacher, particularly when he leads class discussions of cases involving the job of the CEO. His major contribution, however, has been counseling MBA students on careers, always a difficult task even for the trained professional. Some three thousand students have come to him for individual guidance, and many have remained in contact years after graduation.

Having read *How to Turn Your MBA Into a CEO*, I feel Bob Lear's career philosophy is fundamentally sound. With thoughtfulness and proper guidance, an MBA candidate can significantly improve school performance and achieve a high return on tuition investment. In a direct, readable way, he explains how to do this. He is convinced that MBA students tend to do a slapdash job of researching career opportunities and fail to prepare for the best entry-level job.

Lear's wisdom has been culled from years of experience in working for six diversified corporations, extensive board exposure, and from long, close relationship with MBA students. (His office is located in the Placement Division, where some three hundred companies come to recruit each year.)

With an inquiring mind and wry sense of humor, Bob has learned much from other executives and professional career consultants. To a certain extent, however, he is a contrarian: he despairs that too many MBAs are rushing into popular but crowded investment banking or management consulting. Too many block themselves from top management in corporations by taking staff jobs rather than line jobs, where the company must live or die in competition with others. Conversely, too few MBAs take the best courses and seek the best (if unglamorous) entry jobs with companies that lead logically to the top.

I like the recognition Lear gives to individual differences in people's goals, talents, and values, and his students do, too. Four years ago the Graduate Business Student Association at Columbia established the Robert Lear Service Award and made him the first recipient; it is now presented each year at graduation to the staff or faculty member who has been most helpful and accessible to students.

The majority of CEOs will tell you that they never have enough talented, well-educated, motivated young managers in their companies who are acquiring the experience that leads them to the CEO's desk. Of the seventy thousand young people who earn their MBA each year, there are many who have what it takes, but if they do not plan their work at business school and seek the right entry job afterward, they will not be in the right place when opportunity knocks. Bob's career-planning advice is much too good to restrict to Columbia graduates; it can be read profitably by all business school students everywhere.

If you aspire to be a chief executive, *How to Turn Your MBA Into a CEO* is the place to start.

J. P. DONLON

ACKNOWLEDGMENTS

This book could not have been written without the students at Columbia Business School. They have been my examples, my case models, my data bank. For all their problems, and despite their frequent unwillingness to go the way I may want them to go, I have come to admire them and love them.

Equally vital to this book is Elisabetta di Cagno. As editor of the Columbia Business School publications, including *Hermes* magazine, she cajoled me into starting to write my career philosophy into a book, and then helped me complete it.

Because of my rather full work schedules, I wrote almost all of the book in pencil on yellow sheets of table paper in airplanes during business and vacation trips. There I had no interruptions and time enough to work out a series of vignettes.

Ivan Farkas, Ms. di Cagno's secretary, took on the deciphering of my scribbling as a moonlighting project. He put it all onto a diskette and then turned the uncoordinated jumble over to Elisabetta di Cagno.

Some of the basic material in this book is a direct reprint of the handouts given by the Placement Division at Columbia Business School to MBA students to help them prepare for job interviews with recruiters who come to the school. I have included them here with the permission of Dean Frederic Way and his professionally competent staff—Tanya Leslie, Elizabeth Katsivelos, and Michael Sherman. I concur almost totally with what they recommend to our MBAs; my comments are simply an elaboration, an endorsement and an implementation of what they say. And I am indebted to each of them for helping me so graciously in my career counseling activities.

I wish to acknowledge the support I have received from former Dean Boris Yavitz, who first appointed me as Executive-in-Residence with the name of Visiting Professor in 1972, and his successor John C. Burton, who continues to reappoint me each year and who supports my work so totally.

During my stay at Columbia Business School, I have made many friends among the talented faculty. They have invited me to teach their classes, attend their meetings, and share their magnificent school. In similar fashion, the hardworking administration has been continuously and unfailingly cooperative.

My editor at Macmillan, Lindley Boegehold, has been a joy to work with—helpful, positive, and creative.

My secretary at Columbia Business School, Shelley Olson, typed the last few fill-in pages and performed a variety of helpful services.

Finally, I wish to thank those persons who have allowed me to use their names, quotations, or case situations in this book. I wish particularly to thank J. P. Donlon, Editor of *Chief Executive* magazine, for the kind things said in his foreword. And special thanks to Beth Cantor, in association with *AMBA* magazine, for permission to use some of the material found in the Interviewing section.

This little book has taken a lot of time on the part of a lot of people. It has been an interesting project, because

I believe that the MBAs being trained in today's business schools are going to be the corporate executives of tomorrow who will keep American business in a world leadership position. If any of the counsel herein is at all useful in helping our MBAs achieve high performance, then it has been a meaningful project.

Intro-
duction

THE GOLDEN PASSPORT

Some say that the MBA diploma isn't the golden passport to eternal prosperity that it was once cracked up to be. For the top MBAs from the top schools, maybe it still is, but for most of the sixty-five thousand or so MBAs who graduate each year it is gold-plated at best and a costly waste of time at worst.

The leading business schools—that is, the twenty-five or so schools who rank themselves as the top ten—are always going to produce a good return on investment for most of their graduates. They possess a broad curriculum, good teachers, a selective admissions system, an effective placement program, and a useful alumni network. There are certainly some MBAs who slip through the screening process and slide through school into a job situation that is little or no better than what they faced before their school experience.

On the other end of the spectrum, there are MBA diploma factories, usually unaccredited and often heavily weighted with part-time students, who will take almost anyone who applies and can pay the tuition. In a regrettable number of cases, I suspect that the MBA effort of these students was fruitless.

But thousands of highly individual cases are sandwiched in between the upper-caste and the lower-caste MBAs. I know superlative performers who have had the guts and determination to get their MBA at night school and have profited enormously from doing so. The ranks of top executives are packed with people who got their MBAs from small, obscure, or less well regarded business schools.

As a business executive, I like to see an MBA on a résumé, even if it's from Overshoe U. night school. It tells me that the applicant has made an extra effort and has been exposed to a broad range of business subjects.

The MBA diploma or school experience does not in itself guarantee a good job or business success. As it has so often been stated, and correctly, an MBA degree is a license that gives you a chance to find a better job and compete for that job more effectively. It does not get you promoted, nor can it keep you from being fired.

The true benefits of an MBA emerge over a number of years and combine with on-the-job managerial experience. No school can train individuals for executive success. In the end, only you can do it.

WORKING
BEFORE
THE
MBA

Most people usually wait two or three years after their BA before getting their MBA. Your school competition will be more mature. You will have learned the discipline of holding a full-time job. You will have been exposed to organization charts, company communication, corporate politics, and gossip and might even have had some good training that will be useful to you over the long term.

The best kinds of jobs to have between college and business school are those where you are exposed to at least one of the basic business functions: manufacturing, selling, or accounting. A bank job is excellent because you work with balance sheets and money. A job where you are involved with computers is always a plus.

A superb way to accomplish this is to go after one of the two-year internships arranged by some of the large investment banks and management-consulting companies. These firms have specific assignments available that offer productive and interesting work. They are fully aware of the impending MBA move, and hope to attract the best of the interns back after they receive their MBAs. These firms spread the word through the top business schools about their companies and they get a lot of work out of smart young people. There aren't a great many of these slots open—although a firm such as Booz • Allen & Hamilton has about forty people currently in the program—but they are worth scrambling for.

The worst thing that can happen to you by working two or three years is that you can lose your lust for an MBA. You get caught up in the trappings of your work, your social life gets complex, and you get used to a regular paycheck. Maintain perspective by analyzing the differences between MBAs and non-MBAs at your company and in general—who is progressing faster, who has the better training, who is making more money, and who is happier.

It may be worthwhile taking a night school class or two in, say, economics or accounting, to sharpen up your quantitative skills or to be able to bypass a required course in favor of an advanced elective course.

The best thing that can happen is that you find out what you really wanted to learn from your MBA experience. It's a little like the old story of the two bricklayers—one was laying bricks and the other was building a church. Before your MBA classes, you had a job. As you become involved at business school, you will see how your old job fits into the total corporate plan. I have known MBAs to look back on their preschool jobs and say, "My attitude, knowledge, and interest were entirely different then than it would be if I did the same work after my MBA. I'm so glad I worked for a while, but I'm even happier that I got my MBA."

THE CHALLENGE AND THE CHOICE— GETTING STARTED

MBA students in the 1980s have a lot of good things going for them. They came after the difficult period of the Vietnam War, college riots, and rebellion against the business establishment. The majority of the young people who sign up for graduate business schools these days definitely want to have a meaningful career in business, they are anxious to learn as much as possible at school, and they are very competitive as they strive for good grades and search for good jobs.

Am I biased because I have had such a rewarding experience in career counseling? Perhaps so, but listen to this:

I find that my fellow business executives (those characters who are expected to hire you at those fantastic salaries and who have not gotten to know you as well as I have) are inclined to have certain modest reservations about the current crop of business school graduates.

About three years ago, we asked the members of our seven advisory boards at Columbia to tell us what they found lacking or out of whack with business school graduates, regardless of school affiliation, they had hired during the 1970s. They responded thoughtfully and told us they wished we could work on improving four areas in which new MBAs were weak.

- First, *attitude.* Board members told us that too frequently you consider a business degree to be an automatic passport to instant business success. You feel you have learned at school more than your older peers have learned from experience. You are too often intolerant of those who have not acquired your newfound quantitative skills, or who have acquired them at lesser schools than yours. You prefer to talk rather than listen, and you prefer *your* pace, *your* programs, and *your* style to those of your bosses. In short, arrogance was high on the board members' list of negative traits seen in new MBAs.

  I rebut this as gently as I can, saying that these comments are mostly a mental hangover from the perceived attitudes of the late 1960s and the early 1970s, and that as they get to know you, they will grow to love you. Despite this, I urge you to work on being lovable and tolerant and to wait at least a year or two before you demand a vice presidency.

- Second, *ability to communicate.* Board members stated that too many business school graduates are inept at expressing themselves effectively, orally or in writing. Statement: Many business school graduates have not been properly trained in the making of presentations. Observation: They are hence consistently unable to sell a good idea because of sloppy, slipshod communications.

  In a regrettable number of cases, this criticism is justified—regrettable because after all the work and money put into your business degree, blowing a great proposal with a poor presentation is like buying a Halston dress and wearing army boots with it.

Most business schools offer a communications program with videotape machines, for practice interviews; presentation workshops; business-writing sessions; and special seminars on public speaking. If you are deficient in any of these areas, I urge you strongly to sign up for these courses. If they are not available at your school, then enroll in an outside course, such as Dale Carnegie's, that will help you acquire these skills.

· Third, *completeness.* Board members state they see too many business school graduates who are lopsided specialists in finance or marketing or accounting and who do not seem to comprehend fully or care how the whole business fits together and works. They say the deep concentration on acquiring the specialized skills appropriate for an entry job results in neglect of the proper courses that give you a well-rounded, top-management outlook. And they say that newly hired employees are sometimes reluctant to fill those educational gaps.

If you are a new graduate, it's too late now to sign up for those courses in operations management, business law, and strategic planning to round off your sharp angles. But it is never too late to continue your educational program throughout your career. Particularly for those of you who want and expect to be top executives, I urge you to reassess the completeness of your portfolio and fill in the blank spaces.

· Fourth, *career-path selection.* Observation: Almost none of you want to be horses. You want to be the jockey, the bookie, the trainer. You will lend money to the company that builds the racetrack. You will advertise saddles. You will consult with the racing commission.

You will venture capital for a horse breeding farm. You will deal in futures for horse manure.

But you prefer not to compete head-to-head against other horses on the racetracks across the country.

Your job preferences run overwhelmingly these days to positions with professional service agencies, or if you go to work for a corporation, to staff jobs in the headquarters office. You too seldom go after the so-called line jobs in sales and manufacturing which are in operating divisions.

Enough criticism. Let's assume that you have worked hard to develop your interpersonal skills, that you are a good speaker, writer, and communicator, that you took the best courses for a comprehension of the management process, and that you are going to work in the mainstream operating division of a leading corporation. Does this mean that you will automatically become a top-level, broad-gauge, policy-making executive some twenty or thirty years from now?

Of course not. But you have enhanced your odds for success because you will be shooting for ducks where the ducks are flying. You will be where the action is and where those who can manage others for quantifiable results get noticed.

Here are four profound and personal bits of business wisdom that may someday stand you in good stead:

1. There are no pat answers in the cold, cruel business world. In this dynamic society, what was a good or right answer today will probably not be a good or right one for tomorrow.

2. Always volunteer. This is exactly the opposite advice given in the military service. Volunteer to clean up a

mess; to take on an economically hazardous project; to serve on a task force or project team; to transfer to a new and broadening post; to write something; to give a speech. Risk the opportunity for failure—it is an enriching experience, and you will never be in better shape to accept risk than you are right now.

3. Never stop learning. Learn your company's products, markets, and procedures. Learn your next job. Go to night school, to American Management Association seminars, to continuing executive education programs everywhere. Keep on going to school forever. What you have really learned in school so far is how to learn.

4. Become a faithful business school alumnus. Keep in touch with your friends and your faculty. Join and be a working part of the old boy/girl network. Support your school and share its future with yours. It will be a mutually profitable experience.

**REASONS,
REASONS,
REASONS**

MBAs are very good at making up lists of reasons why they like a particular career or why they don't like another.

They are not so good at listing counter-reasons which should be considered before a career choice is made.

Here are four examples of do-it-yourself lists. Three are for careers that MBAs knock themselves out to get and the reasons they do so: corporate finance for an investment banker; management consulting; and consumer packaged goods marketing. The "yellow lights" are my words of caution so you'll look before leaping.

The fourth set of lists is for a career path that begins in the marketing, manufacturing, or control department of the operating division of an industrial corporation. MBAs tend to shy away from these jobs, so I have compiled a list of reasons why these jobs are worth stronger consideration.

Generalizations about industries and companies are dangerous. There are always exceptions and companies are constantly changing. I have hedged a lot of my observations with words such as "most," "many," and "some" because it is possible to find a solid group of companies which run counter to my listings.

The point becomes, then, to make up your own list of positive and not-so-positive factors about the industry areas in which you are interested. Don't kid yourself that *any* job in *any* company is going to be a cakewalk down a daisy-strewn path lined with admiring and generous bosses. There are tough competition, hard work, and difficult problems everywhere. But there are also opportunity and potential rewards waiting in nearly all companies for the MBA who plans his or her work and puts that plan into action.

A CORPORATE FINANCE CAREER
WITH AN INVESTMENT BANKER

Why MBAs Like the Idea	Caution Signals to Think About
High starting salaries	Hyper-competitive field is crowded with top MBAs from top schools.
Possibility of very high incomes after relatively few years of work.	Industry is in turbulent state with many mergers, acquisitions, and power shifts.
Early use of many skills acquired during the MBA program.	
Good acceptance of women for top entry jobs.	Work pace can be incredibly intensive. Long hours, nights, weekends. Lots of number crunching.
Work base is normally headquarters office in metropolitan area.	Many projects are abandoned, lost or unresolved.
Work projects are often exciting and newsworthy.	Most of work is individual or in small teams. Little management or administrative experience is gained.
Creative thinking and action pays off.	
Lots of interesting young peers to associate with.	
Early chance to share profits as partner or senior executive.	Skills learned are not very transferable to other businesses.
Prestige among classmates for selection.	Limited number of partnerships and top jobs available. Very few have been achieved by women or minorities.

A MANAGEMENT-CONSULTING CAREER

Why MBAs Like the Idea

High starting salaries, perhaps the highest anywhere.

Early use of many skills acquired during the MBA program.

Work projects are often extremely challenging and interesting.

Work base is normally at headquarters office in metropolitan area.

Writing and presentation skills are sharpened.

Many clients are famous corporations involved in newsworthy projects.

Exposure to confidential information at high levels.

Contact with top corporate executives.

Lots of interesting young peers to work with.

Chance to make partner at relatively early age and to share in profits.

Caution Signals to Think About

Travel can be excessive. Locations can be unexciting.

Work pace can be intensive. Long hours, nights, weekends.

Many assignments are routine, remote, or unrewarding.

It is frustrating when clients reject or mishandle recommendations and ·work is unresolved.

Most of work is individual or in small teams. Little management or administrative experience is gained.

Specific product and market knowledge obtained is rarely transferable.

Most MBAs who accept jobs with clients' companies go into staff jobs with restricted long-term potential.

| Chance to find uniquely attractive managerial position with client. Prestige among classmates for selection. | Limited number of partnerships available, very few of which are achieved by women and minorities. |

A CONSUMER PACKAGED GOODS MARKETING CAREER

Why MBAs Like the Idea	Caution Signals to Think About
The highest starting salaries for marketing majors.	Field is crowded with top MBAs from top schools. Very competitive. Low job security. High turnover in losing brand areas.
Early use of many skills acquired during the MBA program.	
Excellent training programs.	Much of early work is detailed, quantitative analysis with little room for creativity.
Work projects are usually on high-profile, well-known brands.	
Good acceptance of women and minorities in top entry jobs.	Many of the leading companies are in cities not normally loved by MBAs.
Work base is normally headquarters office in metropolitan area.	Work pace can be very intensive with long hours and, sometimes, excessive travel.

Creative thinking and action pays off. Impact of work can be quantitatively measured.

Ultimate salary progress is slow and depends upon internal corporate policies.

Lots of interesting young peers with whom to associate.

Possibilities of promotion to managerial post after relatively few years of work. Potential route to CEO spot.

Chance to transfer to high-ranking position in smaller company.

Prestige among classmates for selection.

THE OPERATING DIVISION
OF AN INDUSTRIAL CORPORATION

Why MBAs DON'T Like the Idea

Why They Might Be Wrong

Relatively low starting salaries.

Usually excellent training programs.

Many job locations are in unattractive regions and cities and not at head-quarters.

Opportunity to gain early managerial responsibility and experience.

Career success usually involves several moves and transfers and is unsettling to spouses.

Many of the corporations are mature, low-growth, or in prosaic businesses.

Progress in salary and responsibility is long, hard, and slow.

Many companies don't know how to handle fast-track MBAs. Too much chance to get buried or lost.

Without a technical degree, MBAs have a disadvantage in many manufacturing companies.

Lack of prestige among classmates for selection.

Low opportunity level for women and minorities.

Logical start on pathway to top executive positions.

If successful, high long-term salary and incentive prospects are good.

Less competition from other MBAs.

Most companies keep special watch over their MBA hires.

Many companies prefer MBAs without a technical degree.

Many companies have special opportunities for women and minorities.

High transferability of learned skills to other companies.

Good long-term security when successful performance has been achieved.

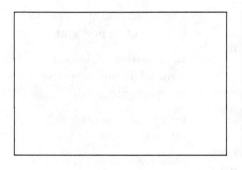

EVALUATE YOURSELF

I'm not much for standardized psychological aptitude tests for business career forecasting. They may be useful in determining whether a young person would make a better priest or mechanic or artist or computer programmer. But I don't know of any test that will help an MBA decide between commercial and investment banking or between consulting work and consumer marketing.

Nevertheless, there are some very basic "aptitude-type" questions that an MBA should ask him- or herself before finally deciding on a career path. A few illustrations:

- Do I sincerely enjoy meeting new people? Do I make friends quickly? Am I an outgoing person?
- Do I really like to write and am I exceptionally good at writing reports? How about speaking and making presentations?
- Is problem solving fun for me? What kinds of problems do I like to work on best? How are my math and quantitative skills?
- Am I well organized and do I like to plan things? Can I switch plans readily to cope with change?
- Do I consider myself a leader, a take-charge person?

Or am I better off as an effective team player and a strong supporter?

- Do I have a lot of creative ideas? Do I like to brainstorm? Do new things excite me?
- How much individual initiative do I have? Am I good at overcoming obstacles? How do I react to failure?

You can make up your own list and make it as long as you wish. Rate yourself on a 1-to-5 basis as objectively as you can.

Then make up a comparable list of the attributes that appear to be most strongly required for success in a particular field. Here are a few examples:

MANAGEMENT CONSULTING Good writer and presenter. Good question asker and listener. Enjoy team problem-solving discussions. Free to travel extensively. Requires three to five years experience.

INVESTMENT BANKING—SALES AND TRADING Outgoing personality. Enjoy meeting new people. Good interpersonal skills. Physically vigorous. Mentally resilient. Competitive. Strong initiative. Like working alone.

INVESTMENT BANKING—CORPORATE FINANCE Good financial problem solver. Creative. Excellent presenter and writer. Tough-minded. Competitive. Physically vigorous. Ready to work long hours. Risk taker.

CONSUMER PACKAGED GOODS MARKETING Creatively inclined. Good at quantitative analysis. Enjoy writing reports and making presentations. Like to work in teams and have good leadership qualities. Have long-range viewpoint.

COMMERCIAL BANKING—LOAN OFFICER Like to deal with lots of reports and data. Good at financial analysis. Enjoy meeting new people. Good reporter. Tough-minded. Want to become administrator.

OPERATIONS MANAGEMENT Enjoy responsibility and authority. Like to work with people. Like to travel; willing to relocate. Mentally resilient. Physically vigorous. Want to become administrator. Have long-range viewpoint.

FINANCIAL ANALYST Good problem solver. Excellent writer, question asker, listener. Like to deal with lots of reports and data. Enjoy travel and working alone.

HUMAN RESOURCES MANAGER Strong interest in people problems. Good listener. Like to deal with lots of reports and data. Good at quantitative analysis. Enjoy teaching and communicating.

ADVERTISING ACCOUNT EXECUTIVE Creative. Good writer. Excellent presenter. Enjoy working with people. Good interpersonal skills. Ready to work long hours. Mentally resilient.

ACCOUNTANT Like quantitative problems and financial analysis. Like to work with lots of reports and data. Good work capacity, both alone and in teams.

SALES MANAGER Like to meet new people. Enjoy travel and relocation. Resilient. Strong personal leadership instincts. Excellent presenter. Quick learner.

Don't take the above shorthand too literally. The world is full of topflight sales managers who were "just fair" salesmen, of excellent financial executives who are not skilled writers, of superb consultants who really don't like to travel. Their drive, perseverance, and other qualities more than made up for all other factors. On the other hand, if you don't enjoy writing, it's foolish to head toward a career that involves huge amounts of report writing. If you are uncomfortable or shy when meeting new people, you are probably not going to enjoy a sales career. If you don't want to fool around with spread sheets and computers, then stay away from financial analysis posts.

It makes the most sense to try for jobs and a career path where your special interests and your particular attributes come into play most frequently. You will be more marketable and you will get more enjoyment out of your work.

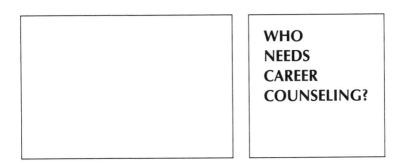

**WHO
NEEDS
CAREER
COUNSELING?**

My business friends ask me, "What is the typical situation you run into as you counsel MBA students on their careers?" There isn't any typical situation. Each is different; each person has unique problems and strong suits. And a student's position changes as he or she proceeds through the MBA experience.

But I have broken the experience into seven distinct time stages when MBAs need to think hard and make decisions which are going to have a lasting impact upon their life's work. Here they are.

1. The preschool analysis.   Should I go to graduate business school at all? Would I be better off staying in my job and taking a few business courses on the side? Or, why not get my MBA at night school? How much and what kind of work experience is desirable before I apply for my MBA? Reviewing my college grades, GMAT scores, and work record, for which business schools should I apply? Given my present thinking as to the kind of life I want to lead, is the major money and time investment in an MBA worthwhile for me? Should I shoot for one of those special two-year internships with a company who knows I will be going for my MBA?

These are tough questions for young people who have had little exposure to business schools or to business itself. Parents, neighbors, and friends are frequently unable to give informed guidance. Admissions officers at school, despite their experience and competence, cannot always effectively fulfill this need for a full discussion on these issues.

2. The first term at business school.   You've decided to get your MBA, have been accepted, and found a way to pay your tuition; now you are bewildered by the confusing array of decisions to be made. What courses should I take? Which ones can I or should I opt out of by examination or by previous college credits? Do I need a refresher course in calculus? Shall I take all the core courses first and defer my electives? Should I try to get certain professors or class times? What shall I put down as my concentration or major—and may I change it later?

Don't sweat it too much during registration. You can get competent help at most schools from the staff and student advisors. Many of the course, timing, and teaching decisions are made for you or are by computer assignment. And, because the core curriculum at most schools is intensive, you'll find that nearly everyone ends up with quite similar schedules for the first term.

However, a wise student seeks counsel on these questions early and begins to think about his or her long-term career.

3. The summer job. Under normal circumstances, MBAs find that a summer job between the second and third terms is highly desirable. But superior summer jobs are hard to come by and the search provokes some difficult questions.

Should I try to get a summer job with the company or in the industry I preliminarily plan to work for? Should I try to get some special kind of experience that fills in a gap? If I can't find what I really want, what are some appropriate alternatives? If I can't get a job through the school, how do I approach it on my own? Is any job better than no job at all? When is it better to go to summer school than to work at a summer job? (*See also* "Those Wonderful Alumni Counselors," p. 47, and "Summer Jobs," p. 49.)

Some business schools—Columbia is one of them—are on the trimester system and therefore start first-term students in September, January, and May. Because summer school is available to all MBAs, the additional option of going straight through is available, and this option justifies special counseling.

4. The "final" functional career choice. By midyear of the third term, the MBA should be deciding on a career path—finance versus marketing versus operations management, for example.

This is an easy task for some MBAs, but for lots of

young people, the decision plagues them all the way to their first job acceptance (and sometimes for many years into their careers). So they need help in coming to a conclusive choice.

Look in the mirror and ask: Which of my courses have held my interest most strongly? What company and industry speakers have given me the sharpest stimulation? Where do I honestly feel I have the best chance of competing? If I gave myself a sincere aptitude test, what would it tell me to do? Can I envision myself building a long-term career in this field and being fulfilled? Which functional career choice most logically follows from my résumé?

5. The "final" business career choice.   As quickly as possible after you have tentatively concluded which functional career path you wish to follow, you should try to decide which kind of business captures your fancy.

For example, if you choose to follow a finance career path, do you prefer investment banking, commercial banking, venture capital, fund management, work in the financial division of a corporation, or one of several other variations on the finance theme? Should investment banking be your thing, do you want to strive for corporation finance work, sales and trading, financial analysis, or one of several other specialized areas?

If marketing is your choice, do you prefer consumer packaged goods, industrial products, business services, market research, or retailing, to name but a few marketing career paths.

It's important to try to make this business career choice early so that you can begin to zero in on the exact companies and jobs you think you'd like. Your preliminary decision can influence the courses you elect to take in your fourth term, the school interviews you apply for, and the outside research and reading you do to prepare yourself for your interviews. It *is* possible, of course, to interview for several different types of jobs with several different types of companies and generate a flow of callbacks and job offers. On the whole, however, the MBAs that seem to be the most successful in their job searches are the ones who have known specifically what they were looking for.

6. The job choice. This is it—and it is usually the most agonizing time an MBA goes through.

Lucky you, with several great offers to pick from. How do I come to the best decision? What comparative weight can I give to company location, salary, short- and long-term opportunity, and so forth? What personal factors must be considered? Which of my specific objectives will be met or missed?

Fairly lucky you, with a job offer or two, but not quite at the hoped-for salary, company, or position. Shall I take a bird-in-the-hand offer or shall I go looking for a bird in the bush? Shall I try to negotiate a better deal or accept what is offered? Why didn't I get more interesting offers?

Poor you, all those interviews and calls and letters, but no job offer and here it is, just a month until graduation. What went wrong that I can correct? Was it my interviewing style or personal approach? Should I reconsider and recast my job objective? I didn't get a job through the school, how do I organize my own job search now?

7. The first few months on the job. You have been hired at that fabulous salary and have that fantastic job you dreamed about at business school.

What obvious mistakes can I avoid? What tips do I
need to do a better job, to be well received, to hop
aboard the fast track? How can I best become successful?

These are some very difficult questions being asked by
MBAs. They deserve careful consideration and a constructive response.

MBAs want to be corporation presidents, management
consultants, venture capitalists, bankers, museum managers, telecommunications marketers, public accountants,
brand managers, real-estate tycoons, international traders,
and entrepreneurs. Each MBA is an individual with a family, school, and work background, highly personal talents,
and goals. Their career aspirations need to be tailored to
their special patterns.

Yet, because they are all MBAs they universally need
to think pragmatically about their careers, prepare themselves for the interviews, and develop an effective approach to the work of their choice.

CAREER MANAGEMENT AT THE HARVARD BUSINESS SCHOOL

Harvard Business School has an interesting course called Career Management. (I wish they had offered it when I was there.)

It is for third termers, and is noncredit, but is one of their most popular courses. I have participated several times in classroom discussions as Professor Jeffrey Sonnenfeld teaches this course.

At a recent session, Sonnenfeld led a case discussion which had to do with recruiting a new chief executive officer for a large corporation. As guest commentators, he had an executive recruiter, the chairman of a large company, and me, representing the director's viewpoint. Each of us was a graduate of Harvard Business School, but about fifteen years apart.

Despite our different perspectives and varying ages, we were able to agree on many things, among them:

1. There is a continuing shortage of executives who have the talent, education, drive, and experience to make them capable of running a large corporation.
2. Relatively few large corporations are doing an outstanding job of developing and training managers for succession to the top posts.

3. It is *much* easier to move from a large company that is a leader in industry to a smaller, related company than vice versa.

4. It is high risk to select an executive with a predominantly staff background for an important line management position.

5. Certain managers achieve executive maturity in a single company through a continuation of work experiences. Other managers develop executive maturity through shifting to other companies every five or ten years. The process depends on the individual.

6. An advanced business education—MBA or equivalent—is going to prove to be an increasingly useful credential for top-executive selection in the next decade.

7. There will always be outstanding top executives who are exceptions to any generalized conclusions about the attributes or backgrounds of successful executives.

Does this mean that, after hearing our erudite conclusions, great groups of Harvard Business School students rushed out to apply for corporate jobs?

Not at all. The largest number of Harvard Business School graduates still go into investment banking, management consulting, venture capital, and other such areas which do not logically lead to senior management slots in industrial corporations—the same way they do at Columbia, Stanford, Wharton, and the other superschools.

They are attracted by the instant gratification lure of the high salaries, early bonus cut-ins, immediate utilization of their MBA skills, and the headquarters locations (mostly in big cities). Why take the long road when the short, fast track is calling?

There are small signs of change. A few more industrial

corporations each year are specifically seeking MBAs for special long-term management development. And a few more MBAs are looking for long-term careers with good companies. Opportunity is knocking here and someone should open the door.

Getting the Most Out of Business School

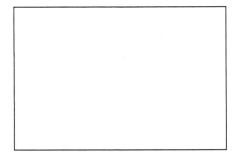

VARIOUS APPROACHES

The several thousand students I have seen getting their MBAs have several hundred different ways of doing it.

There is the "total grind" approach—and the "study-as-little-as-possible—it-still-beats-working" syndrome. There are high-profile activists and those who do nothing beyond the classroom. There are campus introverts and extroverts of all types. What makes sense as a good, balanced way to get the most out of business school?

Here are a few suggestions based on examples of good performance that I have seen in some of our outstanding MBAs.

- Give your classes maximum priority. Don't cut unless absolutely necessary. Make it a religion.
- Go to class as well prepared as possible. From time to time, because of special pressures, you will probably have to risk a skim-through of your assigned material, but make that once in a while. After all, at five thousand dollars a term in tuition, it is costing you forty dollars minimum per class. Get your money's worth.
- Join or organize a study group. Most business problems are best worked out in group discussions. This is especially true when cases are assigned.
- Get to know all your teachers. Make appointments to

discuss your work and ideas with them during their office hours. Go up and talk with them at all social functions and receptions. They know a lot of useful things that don't come up in the classroom. Ask for their opinions on current business stories that relate to the course you are taking. Get them to react to your ideas.

· Get to know your director of placement. Make an appointment and talk to him or her about your career interests—and listen. The director has a wealth of background experience with both companies and students. Use the alumni counseling service to talk about your career ideas before you start on your official interview activity. The placement office usually has a list of alumni who are willing to talk to students about their industries and companies.

· Whenever a well-known business executive comes to campus, go hear him or her speak. When business people come to talk to clubs or seminars, knock yourself out to attend. You will get a wealth of useful tips from these visiting practitioners.

· Join at least two clubs that have programs pertinent to your career interests. Participate in club affairs and make friends.

· Contribute something to the school in the form of a productive activity. Run for office, write for the paper, be a program chairman, organize a seminar. It's good for you, good for the school, and looks great on your résumé.

· Learn how to speak, write, and make better presentations by taking full advantage of communication courses offered.

· Become computer-literate, learn a word processing

program, and become familiar with state-of-the-art
spread sheet and business software. Learn to type fast.
It's an eternally useful skill. Down the line you will be
managing people who type and use computers—obviously you will be a more effective manager if you have
these skills.

- Get to be a whiz at library research. Know how the files
work, how to look up company and industry and financial data. Become familiar with all of the important
resource publications and indexes. Learn how to use
the *BusinessWeek* index; the *Value Line* file; *Standard &
Poor's Register of Corporations, Directors & Executives*; *Who's
Who*; and *Thomas Register of American Manufacturers*. (*See*
"Use Your Business Library," p. 209.)
- Exercise. All schools have an array of athletic facilities
available at minimal cost. Play squash. Swim. Run. Work
out. Play tennis. Try to exercise several times a week.
It's a blues chaser and a fatigue fighter.
- Have fun. Don't miss any of the student parties, *ever*.
Relax and enjoy life when you can. There is so much
work to do that you can get to be a dull and anxious
person if you don't watch out.
- Think positive. Don't be a chronic complainer. Clear
up roadblocks or go around them—it's good practice
for the real world. Getting your MBA is a grand experience. Make the most of it.

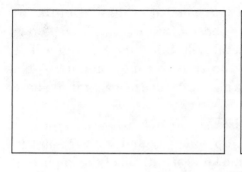

CHOOSING YOUR COURSES

Most of the MBA students I counsel realize I have a strong bias in favor of career paths that lead ultimately to one of the top executive posts at a Fortune 500 company. Because of this interest, I am occasionally asked, "What study path should be taken to most effectively prepare an MBA for success as a general manager?"

1. Take the basics. That means finance, accounting, marketing, and operations management. Making it, selling it, keeping track of it, and financing it are the key elements of the balance sheet, the profit and loss statement, and the vitality of the business. Don't leave school without 'em.

2. Take high-level courses. They are most pertinent to the job of the CEO.

   (a) The best course is business policy. Immerse yourself in the cases and identify with the participants. Follow business policy with a course in strategic planning.

   (c) Take a course in international business. At all large companies today, there's no such thing as a domestic decision. Pick the broadest course that will give you the base for further, detailed comprehension of you future company's multinational role.

   (d) Take business law. The world of business is increasingly enmeshed with lawyers and legal regulations. If you are going to be a manager, you will *have* to deal with contracts, agreements, claims, and suits. Learn about them here first.

Depending on your desired route, take an advanced course in each of these categories: financial controls, marketing, and management of organization. This will require thought and fine tuning to fit into your schedule. (f)

Take a new ventures or an entrepreneur course if you can. It applies best of all to small companies, but provides an excellent microcosm of a large operation. And who knows, you may want to start your own company someday. (e)

The various courses I'm talking about here may not be overwhelmingly useful to you in your first few years. Don't worry. Your curriculum is like a time release cold capsule. Some tablets help right away; others bring relief later on.

3. Opt for a double major.

This could be marketing/finance, finance/real estate, operations/management, or any one of a dozen combinations. It keeps you from typecasting yourself and gives you somewhat more breadth in choosing balanced courses. One of the two should be in the functional area you believe you will probably choose as the primary path for your career.

4. Concentrate on eliminating your weaknesses.

This is the best chance you'll ever have to fill in your gaps. If accounting alarms you, then by all means take cost accounting and financial controls. If marketing mystifies you, then volunteer for a market research or consumer behavior course.

When I go to baseball games, I always remark on the dichotomy of the warm-up sessions. The good hitters are flailing away in the batting cage; the good fielders are snapping the ball around the infield. Shouldn't they reverse roles?

5. Go to the lectures.

Business schools offer a unique and pertinent "course"—the constant series of lectures by visiting business dignitaries. *Standard & Poor's Register of Corporations, Directors & Executives* comes to life right in the lecture hall. These executives are the most successful and most contemporary examples to emulate that exist anywhere, and they are eager to engage you in a spirited interchange.

6. Take a between-terms job.

If you possibly can (preferably between your second and third terms), try to find a job with a company in the industry you think you might want to join when you graduate. It makes your last two terms more meaningful by confirming or dismissing some of your preconceived impressions. It offers a change of pace from four straight terms. And it has positive impact on recruiters. So do it if you can.

On the other hand, if you have already had appropriate job-related experience, if you project a mature and disciplined image, and have a resilient, four-term attention span, then this "course" might not be necessary. We'll give you an exemption.

7. Communicate.

To paraphrase the Duchess of Windsor, "You can never be too rich, too thin, or too good at written and oral communication."

Most business schools have communications programs that provide a superior collection of videotaping equipment, special courses, writing and speaking improvement projects, and talented, professional guest artists. Sign up for practically everything offered. If you're going to be addressing annual meetings, appearing on "Face the Nation," and selling an ice-cold banker on your red-hot projects, then you should learn all you can now about projecting yourself clearly and persuasively. Otherwise, you may never even get to the position of doing so.

8. Get to know your professor.

A business school *is* its faculty, and a course is only as good as its teacher. That's why, when in doubt, you should scramble to get into the classrooms of the best professors first, and be less concerned about the course. This can be overdone, certainly, but it usually makes sense.

The trick is in determining who the best professors are. They may be report-demanding or hard-grading, and thus subject to only fair student ratings, so take these ratings with a grain of salt. A few hours of course research can greatly increase your chances of many happy and productive hours in the classroom.

If you want to communicate with your professors, don't confine yourself to the classroom. Nearly all professors are readily available for office discussion. Many are at their best in informal sessions where the student displays genuine, extra interest.

9. Get to know your fellow students.

If the life of the school is the faculty, then the afterlife of the school consists of the friends you make at school and with whom you will associate over the next forty years or so.

The odds are that a good percentage of the students right now getting their MBAs will become significantly successful in their business careers and *a few* will be notably so. The old boy/girl network is a real and practical asset. It's a virtually cost-free, serendipitous bonus you can get for going to business school. So my last "course" recommendation is to practice your general management teaching at school. Don't be shy, remote, or elusive. Participate vigorously in several clubs. Run for office. Serve on and chair committees. Organize study groups. Contribute constructively to the school. You'll end up knowing more of the high-potential students better and building more meaningful and lasting relationships.

It's amazing how much luckier people who work hard and who are always well prepared are in contrast with those who simply buy a ticket in the lottery. The best time to start your lucky break is right now at business school.

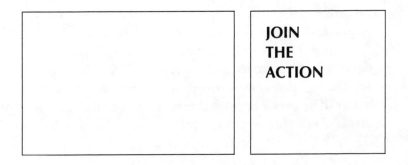

**JOIN
THE
ACTION**

Most top business schools have a strong relationship with the corporate community—MBAs can meet with top executives for career discussion and CEOs regularly speak at seminars and special events. For example, Columbia Business School in New York City, the financial capital of the world, affords a great many such opportunities. Here is an example of a typical week at Columbia Business School. I think of these events as a bonus on your tuition.

WEEKLY ACTIVITIES

OCTOBER 1–5

Date	Time	Activity and Place	Sponsor
Mon. 10/1	5:15–8:00	*General Foods*: "The New General Foods." Charles Borrien, Vice President of the Meals Division, will be speaking.	American Marketing Association
Mon. 10/1	5:30–7:30	*General Electric*: "Leveraging Human Resources." Larry Phillips of GE Aerospace Business Group will discuss current and future trends in Human Resources—ways of improving overall effectiveness and profitability.	Human Resources Management Association

Tues. 10/2	5:30–8:00	*Chemical Bank—Capital Markets Group.* Members of Chemical Bank's Capital Group will cover various aspects of their business.	American Finance Association
Tues. 10/2	5:30–8:00	*Container Corporation of America.* Tom French, Vice President and Regional General Manager—Presentation and Discussion.	American Marketing Association and American Finance Association
Tues. 10/2	5:30–8:00	*McKinsey & Company.*	MBA Management Consultants Club
Wed. 10/3	5:30–8:00	*Goldman, Sachs & Company.* The Equity Division of Goldman's Sales and Trading Department will speak about their approach to business.	American Finance Association
Wed. 10/3	5:30–8:00	*Quaker Oats.* Interested in Product Management as a career? A representative will be speaking about the responsibilities of Product Managers in their firm.	American Marketing Association

Wed. 10/3	5:30–7:00	*Arthur Andersen.*	MBA Management Consultants Club
Wed. 10/3	5:00–7:00	*Columbia Pictures.* Peter Sealey, Executive Vice President.	Communications Management Association
Thurs. 10/4	5:00–6:30	*"War Stories" Panel.* A Panel of 1984 graduates will discuss their Interviewing and Job-Hunting experiences.	Placement and Career Services
Thurs. 10/4	5:00–7:30	*Citibank, Citicorp.* Byron Knief, Vice President, will speak about his experiences at Citibank.	American Finance Association and Banking Society
Thurs. 10/4	5:30–7:30	*Ogilvy and Mather Presentation.* Opportunities in Advertising.	American Marketing Association

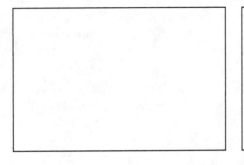

THE HARDEST THING TO LEARN

Business schools today do a pretty good job of teaching MBAs the fundamentals of business—accounting, finance, marketing, organization, etc. The MBA learns how to design decision trees, construct models, and use computers. He or she becomes skillful at problem solving, report writing, and speaking.

The MBA, however, has not been taught how to be a manager. Sure, there were the teaching sessions on management techniques and true-to-life case discussions that dealt with management style, but that's a long way from actually performing as a manager for pay.

In my lexicon, the word "manager" carries the implication that you are responsible for supervising the work of other people and are accountable for their motivation, morale, and performance. This is hard to learn to do and even harder to do well.

The management of people means that you not only must know your job, but also the jobs of the people you supervise. You and they together must agree on what needs to be done by when and at what cost. You must plan and review budgets and schedules. You must appraise performance and redirect efforts when appropriate. You establish controls, maintain communication, and achieve coordination. You cope with problems, accidents, and misunderstandings. You see that all the jobs get done.

Good workers and brilliant individual performers do not always make good managers. The shoals of career channels are strewn with great salesmen who could not become sales managers, great staffers who could not execute, and great planners who could not carry out their plans.

If you truly want to become a good manager—and that's where the power, the glory, and the money are— then you should strive to get yourself into a managerial slot at the earliest possible stage in your career.

There are some things you can do (or have done) in school that will give you early practice as a manager. That's why companies like to interview and hire MBAs who have served as presidents and officers of school groups and so have begun to learn how to get people to work together toward common goals. Useful activities are writing for school publications, leading discussion groups, and organizing student projects of various types.

There are also some things you can learn from courses where team assignments are given, team presentations made, and a team grade generated. The various team members have to find a way to divide and share the work, to criticize and upgrade performance, and to deal with uncooperative or nonconforming partners. It's not the same as working on a project team or task force at a company, but it's close enough to reality to be very useful.

In your job you will learn how to "fly your desk"—that is, handle your paperwork and calls and appointments efficiently, without apparent suffering or strain. You will see firsthand how your various bosses and supervisory associates direct their people and programs—and here you can benefit from both positive and negative methodology. As you rise in the organization, you will add a new layer of managerial wisdom with each exercise in authority and responsibility.

Some of you will become good managers—at least, by your boss's definition, when he or she promotes you. Some of you will take so long to learn the nuances of practical leadership that you will limit your succession opportunity, and perhaps, be directed or confined to staff assignments where you are not immediately responsible for managerial results. All of you will find that you never learn everything there is to know about being a good manager; each day brings completely new challenges which require creative supervision.

Your business school training can make you more receptive to the use of new management tools and methods and more open-minded in trying alternate approaches. In the end, however, you learn to manage by managing and, most of the time, the more you practice managing, the better you learn to do it.

THOSE WONDERFUL ALUMNI COUNSELORS

One of the greatest assets an MBA can have is the alumni network of his or her school. There the alumni are—thousands of them. People who are working for the companies you want to work for. People who understand your circumstances because they were once in your position. People who are astonishingly, almost incredibly, willing to help you plan your career and find a great job.

The older and bigger the school, obviously the more alumni are available for you to talk to. And, of course, the closer your preferred geographical work location is to those of your predecessors, the more chance you have of finding alumni friends. If you are getting your MBA in California and you want to work in Florida, then this advice won't do you as much good as if you were to stay in the West.

Here's how alumni counseling works at most business schools. Periodically, by questionnaire, alumni are asked if they are willing to counsel MBA students who may call them for career advice. A great many agree to do so. From then on, it is up to the student to follow through.

A student may try to talk to a number of alumni who work for several companies in one industry or those who hold jobs similar to the one he or she aspires to, or who have had a similar background to that of the inquiring

MBA. Whenever possible, make your visit in person—the MBA usually gets more time, more information, and more quasi-interview practice than by telephone.

The questions may be candid: What companies in your industry should I think about approaching? What key individuals or people with what titles should I try to see? If I were to approach your company, how best should I go about it? If you could start your career all over again, what different approach might you take?

This is a priceless privilege for an MBA—to be counseled by someone who knows the circumstances and genuinely wants to respond to a courteous young person. An enormous number of job leads have been developed through these counseling contacts. Everyone I know who has used this service claims to have benefited from it.

The one-on-one communication with a businessperson who can give constructive criticism and support is invaluable. Yet my experience shows that only a small percentage of MBAs use alumni counseling, and I find it hard to understand why they don't. Perhaps it is because so many recruiters come to the school for formal interviews that many students confine their job-seeking efforts to that program alone. And, of course, it takes time to look through alumni lists, set up appointments, and make the calls—and a busy MBA never has enough time. I promise you it is worth your while.

It's a shame that not everyone takes advantage of this opportunity, because there is no better way to sharpen your focus for the formal interviewing that ultimately occurs when the job search gets down to brass tacks. The MBA's questions get better and better as the interests become more specific. (*See* Appendix: "Making the Most of Alumni Counseling Board Interviews.")

When an MBA would like to seek alumni counseling in a city or at a company where no alumni exist, how should he go about it? I suggest that the creative MBA invent his own alumni counseling service. How? Students can review the annual reports and various listings of the company that interests them and then write to a specific person in the segment of the business they would like to be in. Send your résumé and say something like this:

> As an MBA at _____(school)_____, I am interested in working for a company in your industry when I graduate. I am not yet applying for a job. Right now, I am seeking information and advice. Would you be willing to give me a few minutes so I could ask you some questions about a career in your industry?

You will get some turndowns and turnoffs, but you will also find that many business executives like to be helpful to young people. They remember very clearly when they were in your position.

SUMMER JOBS

If you can possibly do so, scramble to get a job between the first and second years of business school.

If you are in your early twenties and without significant business experience, it's almost mandatory. It gives you a break from school, gives you time to think about what you have learned, and makes your second year come alive. The best jobs are with firms that have organized, supervised programs where you are assigned to meaningful work. Among my favorite summer employers are commercial banks, management consultants, and the financial divisions of large corporations.

Even if you are between twenty-five and thirty years old and mature and more experienced, you should still seriously consider a summer job. Strive to find a job with a company that is as close as possible to the type of work you believe you want to do when you graduate. It will be helpful to you in your elective courses, will be useful when you start interviewing, and just might produce a job offer.

I know of dozens of students who have ended up going to work for the company that got to know them during the summer. Steve did it in the information sciences division of IBM. Bob worked as an administrative assistant in operations at Air Reduction and went back to them in a field manager position. Lisa and Ogilvy & Mather got along great in the summer and made it permanent eight months later.

These are win/win situations. The company wins because it gets a known quantity that it has tested and liked. The student wins because he or she goes back to familiar ground, with increasing options and an established base of knowledge.

Even when the student does not go back to the summer employer there are still benefits from the experience. More than one student has told me, "I'm glad I took that summer job, even though it wasn't as exciting as I hoped it would be. I now know what I *don't* want to do and I am ready to start thinking in a new direction."

As a general practice, business schools encourage their students to take a "work break" between the second and third terms, which usually falls in the summer. Columbia Business School goes out of its way to extol the benefits of such a program. Here are specific examples of how students react to the summer job experience:

- Andy at American Can. He appraised, in considerable depth, a large group of companies in the retail music and entertainment business which might be candidates for acquisition. He found the job himself through letters, phone calls, and interviews. He had limited previous work experience.
- Gunnar at Nabisco. He worked in the finance division on a broad series of projects ranging from capital authorizations to the annual profit plan. He got the job himself, but used school relationships to help obtain interviews. No previous work experience.
- Harry at the international trade department of Chase Manhattan Bank. Spent most of his time evaluating credit proposals from companies who wished to participate in import/export trading. Got the job lead through the school. A foreign national, he had several years of engineering experience with a large company.
- Katherine at the capital markets group of Prudential Insurance worked on several leveraged buyouts and private placements. Got the job through the school. Had three years of commercial banking experience.

Despite the wide-ranging nature of their summer jobs

and the sharp differences in personal experience, there was considerable uniformity of opinion that:

- The process of thinking about a company to work for and then seeking work there was productive in itself.
- The interviewing exercise was stimulating and highly educational.
- The exposure to workplace reality was invigorating and revealing.
- The secondary associations with other summer interns and with other departments and companies were interesting and valuable.

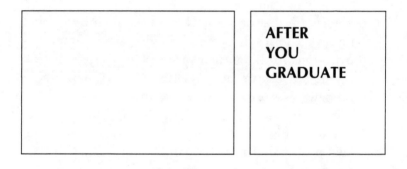

**AFTER
YOU
GRADUATE**

For most of you, it took only fifteen to twenty-one months to acquire your MBA. For some of you, it was simply the end of the beginning of a continuing business education. Distressingly, for others of you, it was a one-shot experience to complete and get over with. If you are in the latter group, you didn't get the maximum return on your investment.

To begin with, the mere acquisition of your MBA should be just the opening salvo to a lifetime program of business education. The school taught you how to learn, gave you a sound theoretical foundation in a number of areas, and tried to tell you that there are a lot more useful things left for you to find out: you didn't learn it all during your business school tour.

What's more, things change. The computer, telecommunications, new legislation, foreign trade, different acquisition techniques, creative marketing, and financial ideas can make your five-year-old MBA obsolete. One way to keep from fading out is to keep in touch with your business school after graduation. Here are a few points of contact to remember:

- Your classmates. You can't keep track of all of them, but you should make a conscious effort to maintain communication with a dozen or so. Organize a joint participation at school reunions. Develop a quarterly newsletter. Make lunch dates. It's worth the effort. You may someday need this network.
- Your local alumni club. Join it and go to the meetings. The speakers are top executives, experts in their fields—discussing state-of-the-art business topics—and the new business friends you meet are stimulating.
- Your teachers and staffers. Go back and see them from time to time, and let them know how you have progressed. Talk with them about your challenges and listen to their ideas. You'll find that you will develop a relationship entirely different from what you had in the classroom.
- Your school affairs. Go back to alumni day, to reunions,

to a lecture, to the annual dinner, to luncheons. It never hurts to show the flag.
· Your participation. Serve on an alumni committee. Help raise money to make it a better school. Offer to teach a class or speak before a club. Act as an alumni counselor. Write an article or a letter for your alumni magazine. Volunteer to become the magazine correspondent for your class. Your classmates will contact you regularly with their news.

The best investment I ever made was in my Harvard Business School education; it has been returned to me many times over. And, because I have maintained a strong and continuous relationship with the school ever since my graduation, the school made an equally sound investment in me.

	SPECIAL CASES

Minority MBAs

Young people of minority heritage frequently find that an MBA gives them the credentials they need to compete

for the best job in almost any company. My career counseling sessions with minority MBAs differed little from
those of other students.

From my teaching and counseling viewpoint, minority
MBAs are generally typical of the student body. The top
third have excellent, well-rounded talents; the middle third
need to work on some facets of their personal portfolio;
the bottom third are scrambling to catch up and hang in
there.

My greatest concern with minority MBAs is that they
allow themselves to be trapped into accepting high-profile
jobs where they would be token representatives or would
be exploited because they were in the black or other minority MBA vanguard.

I'm convinced that MBAs with minority backgrounds
actually have an advantage when they choose a line management route over a staff one. (I think this is generally
true for most MBAs.) There are lots of companies and
individual business executives who are eager to lend an
attentive ear and a helping hand.

That's why, as I talked about careers with minority students, I encouraged Mike to take a selling job with a small
communications firm and was delighted when he got promoted to district sales manager. Here are some accomplishments by minority MBAs: George, who was a class
leader and had his choice of several jobs, made IBM salesman his first pick and is doing very well; Roger signed on
as a brand manager with Frito-Lay; and many other similar
success stories.

The Foreign MBA

As the world of business goes global, it is becoming
increasingly important for all businesspeople to become

familiar with international economics and business practices. In most large U.S. companies there is no such thing
as a purely domestic policy decision. Invariably, in a matter
of any consequence, there are international implications
or complications involved.

The foreign students at Columbia Business School give
class discussions an international perspective. Representing about 15 percent of our student population, they constantly point out the significant differences in managerial
styles, business customs, and legal-corporate practices
throughout the world. It is not enough simply to learn how
things are done in this country.

In the same way, as I talk to foreign MBAs about jobs
and careers, I have certainly come to realize that their
problems are different.

One of the most difficult job-hunting assignments is
that of the foreign national MBA who wants to work in
the United States—and who has only a few months left on
the visa.

Many recruiting companies won't even put foreign nationals on their interview schedule. They have found
through experience that it is too complicated, too expensive, and too risky to invest in a new employee who is in
imminent danger of deportation. Only a few companies
scattered through a variety of industries are willing to put
up with the task of endorsing applications for a longer
stay, particularly since they have no trouble in recruiting
American citizens for their domestic posts which deal with
international affairs.

The foreign student still has alternatives. He or she can
apply for a job in the foreign subsidiary of an American
company, work hard and successfully, and then hope to
be promoted back to the U.S. headquarters of the inter-

national division. An American MBA and fluency in English provide an advantage over fellow nationals.

Another alternative is to go back to your native country, get a job with a company in the industry you would like to work for in the United States, learn the trade well, and reapply for American working papers.

The Working Spouse

The two-income family is part of our way of life today and most well-managed hirers of MBAs have begun to learn how to cope with it.

The working spouse's world is a complicated one, and it takes a bit of effort to arrange two careers in such a way that a reasonable amount of personal time together is achieved.

The most logical approach is for each partner to go after a job with a company whose basic business is located in the same geographical area—commercial banks, investment banks, advertising agencies, management consultants, real-estate firms, and publishers are examples.

In the corporate world, the "nonmoving" type of careers are those in the headquarters office—finance, planning, consumer packaged goods brand management, and a variety of staff functions. Also, of course, if you choose a career with a smaller company that does not have a far-flung business yet, you cut down your chances of being relocated.

This doesn't mean that one or both spouses won't have to travel. There are customers and clients to be seen, projects to be inspected, and meetings to attend. But separation by travel happens to one-income families, too, and it's a part of the experience-accrual, go-get-'em game today.

It is unfortunate but true that some of the best career paths with many of the best companies in the United States usually do involve a lot of moving around. IBM (which the wags say stands for "I've Been Moved"), General Electric, Exxon, DuPont, et al. prefer to have their line managers develop their skills in a variety of areas and posts. The person in sales who is on the way to become vice president of marketing will serve time in several district offices and field divisions. The operating manager will be stationed at multiple manufacturing locations. The division president has to locate where the division is. (I had an easy time of it and moved my family only three times; most of my fellow CEOs had five or six moves.)

So life becomes a trade-off when a promotion is offered and a move is involved. The offer can be refused, to be sure, but in many cases such a refusal can jeopardize a career. Or, one working spouse accommodates the other and tries to work out a simultaneous relocation. It can be done, but not without a strain on the marriage.

The time to think these problems through is early enough in the career so that one or both partners can develop a transportable skill and go along—or decide on careers that are geographically stable.

A good example might be for one marriage partner to become an experienced auditor for a Big-8 accounting firm. Such a firm has offices in every major city in the country (plus a lot of international ones). If one is transferred from, say, New York City to Denver or Houston or Milwaukee, the auditor spouse can generally arrange his or her own transfer pretty quickly—or can find a variety of other local accounting firms to talk to. To a degree, the same transferability exists for a person who has learned a trade in retailing, brokerage, advertising, commercial banking, construction, management information services, and many other businesses.

In addition, there is the matter of maternity or paternity leave. There is a time to pull out of the work force to have and rear children.

I know some MBAs who have been so dedicated and resilient that they have managed to take the minimal maternity leave and go right back to work. But more MBAs prefer to pull out for two to five years and they ask, "What kind of a job can I seek that will give me the least penalty for my absent time?"

Again, I think there are a lot of jobs that fill this bill neatly: As a financial analyst for an investment firm, for instance, you can keep on top of your field through reading at home, plus occasionally attending meetings and conventions. You do not lose your expertise; upon returning, it is not too difficult to catch up with the new trends, new products, and new people: you missed very little.

Our accounting example is much the same. It is possible here also to keep informed on current trends through reading. It may also be feasible to come back on a part-time basis—for the January to April crunch, perhaps, or working from 10:00 A.M. to 3:00 P.M. for a while.

An advertising career person, once having developed a record of successful campaigns and satisfied clients, has a highly portable portfolio to take to another city or to bring back after a layoff. A broker who has once learned how to serve customers effectively can replicate the experience without undue sweat. A skilled salesperson who has developed the ability to persuade people to buy a product or a service is rarely going to be out of a job for long. If you just think about it, there are loads of jobs which blend in well with the working spouse approach.

Unfortunately, the *hardest* jobs to take time off from and to transport are the line jobs where you are a player on a team, where someone has to fill in for you, and where you are involved in a cumulative, learning, and maturing process. Some enlightened companies, on the other hand, do make special efforts to fit leave-taking in the picture. During interviews, it is perfectly fair to ask about leave policies and to find out if there are some good examples at the company of successful executives who have taken a significant leave and then returned to work.

Gray Panthers

These days, a great many MBAs are twenty-seven or twenty-eight years old when they graduate—that's about average at Columbia Business School, for instance. They have taken between two and four years after college and before business school to pursue other interests.

Balancing out the average, however, are a number of students in their mid to late thirties who waited longer before starting business school.

Because the average student is younger, if you are a bit older it may be a surprise to the recruiter, who will wonder why you waited so long to get your MBA. Perhaps the recruiter thinks you are too old to take the company training course. The older MBA does not fit the preconceived pattern of candidates. So, when the recruiter makes up the callback list, some of the most attractive "gray panthers" are often left out.

Placement offices work very hard with recruiters to educate them about MBA demographics. They are making some progress, but the fact remains that the thirtyish MBA has a harder time getting a job than does the twentyish MBA.

What can be done about it? Here are some suggestions:

First recognize that you *are* different and quit trying to hide in the crowd. Most often, your work experience was not of a profit-seeking nature—you taught school, served in the Peace Corps, worked for the government, produced plays, ran a museum. Try to capitalize on these experiences, which have given you a broader perspective and a fuller understanding of interpersonal relationships.

Second, exploit the positive things you have learned— leadership, responsibility, human relations, speaking, and so forth. Don't wait for the interviewer to dig them out. Present them succinctly and positively.

Third, emphasize your maturity. You now know what you want to do, you have stable values, you are prepared to make a long-term intelligently considered commitment. Sell this asset vigorously.

Fourth, be prepared to find your own companies to interview. The people who come to business schools to recruit naturally have established patterns for their MBA hires to fit into. Those hundreds of good companies who do not usually hire newly minted MBAs may be pleased to talk to someone else with your attributes.

Fifth, realizing the above four points, you should begin early to plan your career alternatives and to develop your personal marketing plan.

A thirty-two- or thirty-four- or thirty-six-year-old with a new MBA isn't old—just mature enough to recognize how much more he or she can contribute to an employer—and confident enough to sell that attribute.

Career
Strategy

ABOUT SUCCESS

When an MBA says, "I want to be successful" I ask him or her to define success. This usually results in some stumbling around.

"To make as much money as I need to do the things I want to do . . . to have a good job that I like . . . to go as far as I want to go in a company . . . to feel I have achieved something worthwhile . . . to be both rich and happy, I guess." These are the answers I get most frequently.

To some MBAs, success appears to be equated with a monetary goal, or with a point on the corporate pyramid. This is a short-sighted viewpoint because success cannot be a destination. One never really reaches it, because there are always further goals and changing objectives.

Instead, success is a journey. One should aspire to perform each task in a successful manner, to make each job a success, to be judged by his superiors, peers, and subordinates as a successful manager—and ready to move on to success in another more challenging and rewarding venture.

When you finally decide upon a specific career and when you are considering the company that will supply you with a potential path to success, spend a little time thinking through your personal definition of success.

Be flexible about it. Your definition will change as you change, so set a series of short-term goals that can give you a sense of achievement as you reach them—like climbing ridges as you head for the top of the mountain. Stop occasionally to admire the view and reassess your route.

You may, in time, reverse your long-term goals as you weigh the sometimes conflicting priorities of family, health, happiness, and personal values. You may discover that your talents and your ultimate interests lead you on a different path to a new definition of success.

I have known many high-ranking executives who felt that they really never achieved "success" even though they made a great deal of money. Conversely, I have known many lower-level executives who achieved success in their mind's eye as they became respected professionals in their selected fields of endeavor.

Remember always that success is not a destination, but a journey. Have fun along the way.

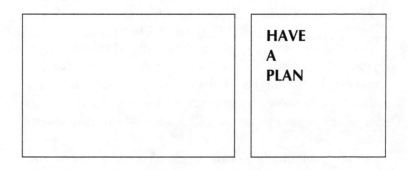

At graduate business school, most MBAs take a course in strategic planning. They learn how a company or a business unit sets long-term goals—how big and how profitable it thinks it can become, what businesses it wants to be in, what strengths it can capitalize upon, what weaknesses it must overcome, and what specific action needs to be taken to make the plan work.

As a personal business unit, an MBA should have a strategic plan, too. Try to identify as clearly as possible what you would like to be doing at the peak of your maturity, energy and earning power, around age fifty.

At first, this will be a fuzzy vision, so indistinct that the only merit involved in thinking about a plan is in the exercise itself. Gradually, however, just as companies do, the MBA should each year redo his strategic plan. After a while, the vision will begin to clear and the steps required to accomplish the goal will be increasingly obvious.

Sometimes the entire strategic plan will be radically changed. (This happens to companies, too, when a merger takes place, or technology shifts, or new competition arises.) Don't be alarmed. Instead, modify your plan to cope with the new environment. Continue to build upon your strengths and overcome your weaknesses. Keep an attainable goal ahead of you all the time. And keep working logically and inexorably toward achieving it.

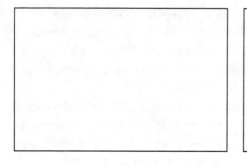

HOW TO BECOME A CEO

There are six logical routes to the job of CEO at a company:

> Inherit it.
> Marry it.
> Buy it.
> Start it.
> Be recruited for it.
> Grow up through the ranks.

There's nothing wrong with any of these ways. It helps, in the first two cases, to have picked the right parents or the right spouse. It helps, in the next two cases, to be rich or entrepreneurial. But most CEOs take the last two routes. In these cases, the new CEO was chosen because he had developed a track record of tangible achievement. If you wish to be a CEO someday, start building the right kind of track record as soon as possible.

When should you start thinking about becoming a CEO? It's never too soon. If you have any leanings in this direction, you should take courses in business school that cover the maximum range of the management spectrum. Go to lectures given by CEOs. Learn to think like a CEO.

When you select your first job, it is not out of line to

fantasize a career path at that company all the way to the top. Ask what routes the last two or three CEOs traveled. Ask yourself if your first step is a logical one.

As you work effectively at your job, you will be offered promotions and transfers to new positions. Are these forward steps on the right road, or are they diversions, detours, or blind alleys? Occasionally, it is wise to turn down an offer if you have a good reason. The important thing is to think about the CEO job while you are still in your twenties and thirties and not wait until you have drifted off course. Don't miss the boat because you started from the wrong dock.

One of the major reasons I encourage MBAs to work for a corporation is that it gives them a chance to become the chief executive officer. In rebuttal, my students sometimes ask, "Is that really a worthwhile target? Isn't the road so long and job so difficult that there isn't enough satisfaction when I get there?"

Yes, it does take a long time; the typical CEO of a Fortune 1000 company is in his fifties when he makes it. It is difficult and demanding work; few people can tackle it and even fewer ever master the job. It does not have guaranteed security. If the company fails to perform under his aegis, the CEO, more so these days than ever, is in danger of being removed from the job by the board of directors.

On the other hand, the rewards for being an effective CEO are absolutely marvelous. Material rewards include a salary and bonus usually well into six figures, with million-dollar-plus annual incomes becoming commonplace. The perquisites and trappings of office can be princely; a company plane, a chauffeured limousine, and a full support office cannot be overpraised. The potential for extremely lucrative capital gains through realizable stock options is waiting for the CEO who can make the company grow during his or her tenure. And the opportunity to serve as an outside director on the boards of other companies is topping on the CEO cake.

But those are material things. They are a critical part of the reward system but most CEOs have just as much or more interest in two other things that go along with the CEOs job.

One is power. The CEO is the boss, even though he or she reports to the board and is responsible to the shareholders. The CEO can and must make decisions that have great impact on the company's present and future success. The CEO influences the buying and selling of major business segments; hires, fires, and realigns key executives; has impact on the company's products, markets, and policies. As Harry Truman said: "The buck stops here."

The other is excitement. The CEO's job can be and usually is fast-paced, fast-changing, and fast-track. The high-profile CEO deals with important people in industry and in the community in confidential, delicate, and controversial matters.

Practically every CEO I have known, including me, genuinely loved the job and thought it was worth fighting and waiting for. Try for it. It might suit you to a T.

MANAGING A PROFIT CENTER

The first goal an MBA should shoot for is to get into a job where the results can be measured quantitatively, preferably through managing others, and ideally through managing a profit center.

The manager of a profit center is a boss with a plan, a budget to supervise, and specific targets to achieve. It involves dealing with several disciplines—manufacturing, marketing, and control for example. There are limits to authority, so he or she must deal effectively with others, and must learn to use staff services. The manager must delegate authority to staff people but realize that accountability can never be delegated.

Once having accepted the responsibility of running a profit center—and effectively met the goals set by the boss—the MBA should be able to see clearly what the opportunities are, meeting and exceeding specific goals and thus embellishing his or her track record. The MBA can do a better job of planning, developing, communicating, and coordinating, and can learn how to manage people, time, paper, problems, and procedures—learn by doing it wrong and then by doing it right the next time. The MBA can make the profit center grow and automatically be in the running for promotion to manage even larger and more complex centers.

To run a profit center is a marvelous management exercise. It forces the MBA to use virtually all the business school courses and to call on all of the personal skills.

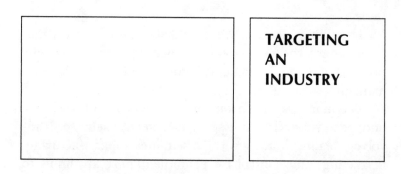

**TARGETING
AN
INDUSTRY**

Over the years I have had an astonishing variety of questions and problems brought to me by MBA students who want to talk about their careers. (Each of the twenty-five hundred or so students I have talked with is unique and I have never found two identical situations.) However, there is one recurring situation that has come up several hundred times. It goes something like this:

Student: "I'm embarrassed to tell you that I am finishing the third (or second) term of my MBA and I still haven't made up my mind as to what kind of a job to go for."

Lear: "That's neither abnormal nor unusual. However, the time is approaching when you should come to some preliminary conclusions. What general avenues have you been thinking about?"

Student: "I have a joint concentration in marketing and finance, so I want to take one of those routes. I know that I don't want to go into consumer packaged goods marketing nor do I want to go into either commercial or investment banking. I *think* I'd like to work for a company, but probably not one of the great big ones."

Lear: "Then why don't you slant your career toward a medium-sized or smaller company in either a marketing or financial entry job?"

Student: "I don't know how to go about it. I don't know that much about such companies. They don't come here to the school for interviews. What should I do?"

Lear: "Get to work on it."

Here's how. Weed out the industries you don't want. Decide on the geographical region you'd like to work in. Begin to make a list of industries or types of companies that have interested you or products that you might enjoy being associated with.

Arbitrarily, pick a sample industry group. Let's say the ideal company you seek is a medium-tech, a product manufacturer rather than a service company, has between 100 and 500 million of sales and is located in New Jersey, New York, Connecticut, Rhode Island, or Massachusetts.

Then zero in on some specific industries and companies. Get the leading trade magazines in those industries and read the advertisements and articles. Force yourself to make up a list of twenty-five companies you think may interest you.

Go to *Poor's* or *Value Line* and pull a summary story for each company. Then, get a copy of their annual reports —from the library, your broker, or from the company itself.

Winnow your list down to the most promising companies and areas. Re-sort and reclassify by new groupings and perhaps add some new companies.

Start your field work. Go through the alumni counseling service and find friendly people in some of these companies to talk to in depth. Write letters and try to get appointments to see as many companies as you possibly can.

Rather than simply sitting back at the school and waiting hopefully for recruiters to come to you, use your initiative and drive and creativity—in the meantime you will also learn a lot of useful information and skills.

Many of the companies you contact will not have a formal MBA hiring program. They may have had previously unhappy experiences with MBAs in recruiting or hiring and you have to convince them that you are different. They may normally recruit MBAs only on the rebound from their first job with another company. They may not have any open positions and need to be sold on the idea of hiring you. And yet some of the very best jobs that any MBA will get are those with companies that they have personally sought out.

Most MBAs shy away from taking this approach the first time around. They feel it involves too much work, even though the basic library research takes no more than a couple of days. They indulge in wishful thinking that a shortcut will appear in some mysterious way. Or they keep procrastinating until they are caught up in the formal recruiting process and simply go along with a herd that they don't fit into.

When they do not come up with the job of their choice—or even more poignantly, when they are deciding to leave their first ineptly chosen job—then MBAs are much, much more amenable to undertaking a serious and thoughtful program of finding the right job. Why wait until that point? Get it right the first time.

CHOOSING A COMPANY

How wonderful can life be? As a soon-to-be MBA, it is not at all unusual to be offered several jobs by different companies. This is a wonderful problem to have, but most MBAs agonize as they weigh one offer against another. Many of my counseling hours have been spent with my young friends as they go through the painful process of trying to come to the best decision.

Because selecting the right entry job is so important, we're going to spend a lot of time talking about this decision and we will get into details later on. To start the discussion let's look at a list of *logical factors* to be considered by an MBA in choosing the company he or she wants to work for.

Here is a list of twelve items, with twelve questions to ask yourself. Just for fun, grab a pencil and rank them in order of importance to you in making your final choice. Then read on and see whether you agree with me or not.

QUIZ CONTEST

LOGICAL FACTORS IN CHOOSING COMPANY OFFERS
IN ALPHABETICAL ORDER

Your Rating

———————— 1. Career path clarity. Can I see where I can go and grow in the company, and does it appeal to me?

———————— 2. Compensation. How much am I being offered and how often are salary reviews conducted?

———————— 3. Fast track. Does the company have special provisions for handling MBA progression separately from a standard pattern?

———————— 4. Financial conditions. What is the company's present and potential financial strength versus its competitors'?

———————— 5. Geography. Where will I live and how will I like it?

———————— 6. Growth trend. Has the company grown effectively in the right areas and what are its continuing prospects?

———————— 7. Industry economics. What is the outlook for the industry I'm thinking about entering, and is it the right one for my long-term career?

———————— 8. Market position. To what extent is the company a leader, and is its position threatened?

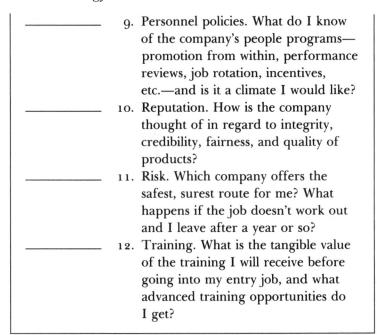

9. Personnel policies. What do I know of the company's people programs—promotion from within, performance reviews, job rotation, incentives, etc.—and is it a climate I would like?

10. Reputation. How is the company thought of in regard to integrity, credibility, fairness, and quality of products?

11. Risk. Which company offers the safest, surest route for me? What happens if the job doesn't work out and I leave after a year or so?

12. Training. What is the tangible value of the training I will receive before going into my entry job, and what advanced training opportunities do I get?

If you are having a little trouble in filling out your rankings, don't be disturbed. To begin with, you haven't gone through the process of recruiting and interviewing, so you are dealing with intangible situations; they will become real soon enough for you.

More to the point, these are tough questions, even after you have tried to obtain all the facts and have talked to all the people who can help you. The answers to most of the questions lie in the future—how well you perform, how efficiently the company is managed, and how competitive the industry turns out to be. As we all know today, and as the stock market proves, it is hard to predict what's going to happen next week, much less in the next couple of decades.

In truth, there isn't any simple set of rankings or ratings that could apply to all MBAs because each person's circumstances, values, and goals differ greatly.

Elena, for example, had an overwhelming priority on geography. Her husband had just joined a law firm in Miami and that is where she wanted to go. All other items became of secondary consideration.

Or take Rick. He wanted to get overseas marketing experience and was willing to make many compromises to come up with the job that gave him that background.

I feel the overriding element to look for in a company to work for is quality. If you can find a company that defines quality the same way you do, and can demonstrate to you that it practices what it preaches, then you are a long way toward deciding where you want to work, and all of the rest of the pieces begin to fall into place. Not only huge corporations have quality; fine jewels often come in small packages. The trick is to determine how to match your skills and interests with the company, then consider the quality factor and sell yourself to them. And that's what we'll be talking to you about.

In the list of twelve factors above, I have purposely included these two red herrings:

✱   The *risk factor*: So many students worry about risk, and unduly so. I encourage MBAs to face up to a certain amount of carefully measured risk, especially when the corresponding reward ratio is good.

✱   The *compensation factor*: This is really a sore point with me. If I had my way, it would not be included on any lists at all. When *all* of the other factors are properly reviewed, the matter of compensation can then be addressed with discretion.

Over the course of his or her business career, a competent MBA will earn hundreds of thousands, even millions of dollars. To choose one company over another because of a starting salary difference of a couple of thousand dollars is short-sighted. Most good companies (I can almost say all) try to be competitive in their salaries, particularly in early management positions. Lesser companies often feel they must offer higher salaries to attract highly qualified young people.

In my career-counseling interviews, I will not allow the subject of salary to come into discussion. When a good job has been done of analyzing the credentials of a prospective employee, the question of starting salary usually answers itself.

WHAT PROCTER & GAMBLE, GENERAL ELECTRIC, AND GTE THINK ABOUT MBAs

Wallace Abbott, a senior vice president at Procter & Gamble, tells me that his company believes that young people today want to work where they:

1. Are given responsibility early.

2. Can assume some degree of risk along with responsibility.
3. Have a meaningful voice in the decision-making process.
4. Feel free to express their feelings about their jobs and their company.
5. Can work in an environment suitable to self-development.

In recognizing these desires, Procter & Gamble in turn realizes that these aggressive young people need more information and communication than might normally be put forth. As a result, senior supervisors meet frequently with them during their first few years of employment and discuss their ideas and problems.

It is an enlightened attitude such as this that helps to make Procter & Gamble one of the corporations that MBAs love to work for. There are many others who feel the same way, but there are some who don't.

I don't work for General Electric nor do I have any material relationship with them. However, I admire the way they state their principles, hire good people, and then train and develop managers.

I recently heard Jack Welch, GE's dynamic chairman, speak, and his observations were candid and refreshing. Here are some of the things he said, which have been repeated in GE's annual reports and recruiting literature:

- We [General Electric] are advancing a competitive culture that has a sense of urgency, that demands the very best, and that emphasizes how crucial an individual's contribution can be to the success of our enterprise.
- Our goal is to expand the climate for excellence, to

create an atmosphere where more and more people do what even they thought they couldn't do.

- We want men and women who create a spirit of can-do and agility in difficult atmospheres where the reality of the marketplace causes the competitive juices to flow.

John Reinsberg, a recent graduate, is quoted in "GE for MBAs" (General Electric's recruiting brochure). He says, "My MBA training and language skills have been real assets [in the Trading Company]. These tools allowed me to jump right into my first assignment and have given me the framework on which to hang my working experience at GE. GE wants you to get the overall picture and broaden your experience base. As a result, you move around through various assignments. You also get the chance to participate in specialized development courses and activities."

GTE, in Stamford, Connecticut, is famous for its telephone companies and its telecommunications equipment. It is also famous for the way it hires topflight young people, trains them on a fast track, and injects them into its organizational system.

They call their system the Associate Development Program. Each year they recruit about ninety people for the program with half or more being MBAs.

For one and a half years, these associates (as they are called) are rotated through a variety of jobs in GTE operating divisions across the country. They are given written evaluations every three months.

At the end of the eighteen-month period, each associate writes out a summary of his or her experiences in the program and outlines some preliminary job objectives. These reports, together with their résumés, are then circulated throughout the company and, following further interviews, the associates are placed in job assignments.

As this program has been in effect since 1973, the company has become adept at handling, measuring, and maximizing the value of newly hired MBAs. And now you now why they say, "Gee. No, GTE!"

Just because I quote Procter & Gamble, GE, and GTE doesn't mean there aren't dozens of companies who have substantially the same attitude and approach and who would be just as wonderful to work for. For example: Bristol-Myers, DuPont, Mobil, Exxon, General Mills, General Motors, Air Products and Chemicals, Chemical Bank, Dayton-Hudson, Ogilvy & Mather, 3M, Boeing, Morgan Guaranty, H. J. Heinz, IBM, Xerox, Monsanto, Arthur Young, McKinsey, Goldman Sachs, Coca-Cola, Time, Dun & Bradstreet, and many more. It's worthwhile looking for them.

**GET ON THE
MAIN TRACK
AND LOOK
FOR THE
WELL-WORN
PATH**

In this age of diversification and conglomeration, most companies are now in a variety of businesses. They try to find off-setting economic cycles, cash flow balances, new growth situations, a complete line of services, and greater integration. That's why DuPont buys Conoco, General Motors buys Hughes, and American Express buys a bank. Almost invariably, however, there is still a core business that serves as the heart of the company and acts as the mainstream for manager development.

Just as invariably, the top executives of the company have come up through the ranks of the primary business, or have had solid exposure there. If you want to be the chairman of Mobil, plan your career route through the petroleum business, and not the Montgomery Ward division. If you want to succeed at Coca-Cola, the best route is probably through the beverage division rather than their company Columbia Pictures.

However, this can change. For years, the top management at General Electric usually had a tour of duty in the electrical apparatus group; right now, the General Electric Credit Company might be as pertinent. Allied-Signal, once a dedicated chemical complex, is now a broad-line industrial complex. U.S. Steel, once the steel industry leader, now has the largest part of its business in energy.

There are rarely any hard and fast rules in a company for particular talent paths, but there are loads of cases where so many executives have followed the same route that it has become a well-worn path.

At Procter & Gamble, president after president has a marketing background, usually as a major-brand manager; if you are a manufacturing or financial executive, no matter how great, you are bucking the wrong odds at P&G.

At IBM, the standard starting job for the CEO race is in sales. At General Motors, the president comes through manufacturing, and the chairman through finance. At Texaco, the preferred path starts with the drilling rig. At

Turner Construction, you were a building project leader and then a territory manager. At ITT, when Harold Geneen was the boss, the favorites were the outstanding controllers. At Texas Instruments, the design engineers have it made. At Bloomingdale's, it's the buyers.

There are lots of exceptions. Every week or so, an interesting story is written about a new executive who made the grade in a different way—an accountant becomes the head of a steel corporation or a soft drink marketer is recruited as president of a computer company—but these are exceptions and that is why they are so newsworthy.

TWO MYTHS EXPLODED

"I don't want to go to work for a large company because:

1. There are too many talented people fighting for too few jobs at the top.
2. It is too easy to get lost or trapped."

The top executives of large companies frequently tell me that one of their continuing problems is the *shortage* of young managers with the talent and drive to reach the higher executive echelons in their companies.

The chairman of the Mobil Corporation, for example, told me that the executive committee of his board of directors recently held its annual corporate personnel review. An appraisal is made each year within Mobil to pinpoint those managers who are expected to have the ultimate potential to rise above a specified salary range—where the top one hundred or so Mobil executives are situated. He was concerned that only twenty-five "executive comers" had been placed on this list.

Similarly, the chairman of General Electric sets aside the August board meeting each year for an appraisal of the company's management development situation. Policies and programs are discussed, together with a review of the potential successors for the upper-level management jobs. And, according to the chairman, "there are never enough real comers" despite the company's acknowledged special efforts.

One of IBM's greatest strengths is its overall, in-depth performance appraisal program. Every manager is a talent scout for outstanding young managers, and one of the primary marks accorded to a manager is his or her ability to develop more managers. A top IBM executive told me, "Almost from the day we hire a person, we begin looking for those attributes which indicate long-term leadership potential. When we find a person who shows good signs, we begin the long, long program of job rotation, task-force work, secondary training, and promotion. We like to know where our good people are and how they are progressing all the time."

These are but three examples of fine companies who dedicate themselves to finding and developing future managers—and there are several hundred other companies who have carefully crafted management development programs with similar purpose and priorities.

There will be some MBAs who end up in an industry or company that falls behind the overall compensation parade. There will be MBAs who feel they are being moved too slowly or who run afoul of a boss who does not fully appreciate them. There will be MBAs who lose out to others in the race for a specific post.

But lost in the crowd? Overwhelmed by too many genuine fast traders? Very rarely does it happen, and then it is usually a temporary situation that affords a new and interesting experience for the competent MBA worker.

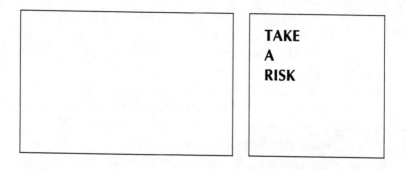

**TAKE
A
RISK**

MBAs often feel that they should make a conservative choice in a job. They believe it is prudent to be especially careful in assessing all of the potential risk factors in each case, and then to choose the safest option.

But learning when to take a risk is important. When you are in your twenties, with no children, no mortgage, no college tuition bills—that's the best time in your life to take a job risk. If it doesn't pan out, then you probably had a marvelous experience that will stand you in good stead forever, and you can go out and find a new, more traditional job. You may have temporarily lost a little time and money, but if the risk to reward ratio was a good one, then it was probably worth taking a crack at.

Take a chance on going with a new, small, struggling company with exciting ideas about genetics or software or telecommunications. Take a chance on a turnaround situation (à la Chrysler), a decaying business (a steel company), a runner-up in a dominated industry (a computer manufacturer other than IBM), or a spin-off from another company, the product of a leveraged buyout. Take a chance on going with an entrepreneur or a maverick or a contrarian of some sort. Take a different type of job than most of your classmates are seeking. Take a job that has a low starting salary but has the possibility of a high payout if certain things happen.

Your MBA will perform a little bit like an insurance policy here. It gives you a good basis to evaluate a risk before undertaking it. And it will help you to cope with the unexpected situations you will be running into. Finally, if your risk was miscalculated for any reason, your MBA training will help you find a new job more quickly.

Why be dull, routine, parochial, provincial, or traditional when you can be creative and original?

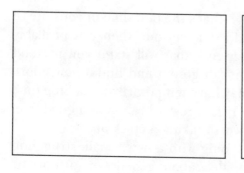

BE
LUCKY

The best way to be successful in your job is to develop your skills so that you always do your assigned work better than anybody else. That's important. But it's essential to be lucky—lucky enough to be in the right place at the right time. When Frank Cary, chairman of IBM, spoke at Columbia a few years ago, a student asked, "You have the top job in the most successful company in the world. To what do you attribute your success?"

The candid query provoked a burst of laughter, but Cary's answer was serious. "I was lucky enough to be in the right place at the right time—it helped a lot to start as a salesman for IBM when its sales were only $400 million. But I have to add that I competed head-on for promotions twenty times and I won each time."

I've been lucky a thousand times in my life—lucky to get my MBA, lucky to be offered several good jobs, lucky to have had great people work for me, lucky to have stock options pay out, lucky to negotiate successful contracts. And I've seen lots of my business friends be lucky, too, like Frank Cary was.

 It's surprising, though, how much luckier those people who work hard and who go out and knock on doors are than those who wait for opportunity to knock on their door.

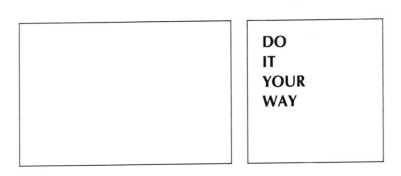

**DO
IT
YOUR
WAY**

Occasionally, a student will say, "You keep telling us that, if we want to have a successful corporate career, we should go to work as soon as possible in a marketing, operations, or a control job in a line operating division. That may have been the way to do it and it may still be for a while longer in some companies. But things are changing. We've got computers, fiber optics, and robotics. Planning, financing, controlling, and communicating are greatly different than they used to be and more changes are coming. Company cultures and structures are changing dramatically. Are you sure that I need to work in the plant or sell in the field in order to have a successful corporate career and, ultimately, qualify for the top executive positions?"

That's a long and reasonable question, so I'll try to give a long and reasonable answer. Things *are* different in the corporate world these days and there has been a real impact upon corporate-career pathways. However, as I see it, the changes now being wrought are opening up new roads without closing off any of the old ones.

Let's look at a few of the current road maps:

THE FINANCIAL ROUTE

There is no question that the finance division in corporations is far more important than it used to be and that, in turn, corporate-financial executives carry far more clout and have much greater range. Global expansion, high interest rates, complicated loan structures, sophisticated debt vehicles, computerized management information systems, and sheer size have forced companies to find and develop senior financial executives who can manage cash, credit, and people. So they have greatly expanded their financial divisions and are recruiting more MBAs for their staffs.

These MBAs have two growth routes open to them. One is to learn as much as they can about the company, its products, and its markets, establish a reputation for good work, and then manage to be transferred to a finance-oriented post in an operating company. But let's concentrate on the other growth route, which is within the finance division itself.

There are lots of good jobs in the finance division of a large company that fully utilize MBA skills, stretch the MBA's problem-solving capabilities, and have measurable impact on the profit results of the corporations. The range can be from working on new borrowings, participating in acquisitions, analyzing problem situations anywhere in the company, managing cash and investments, and producing financial reports.

In a typical company, the treasurer, controller, and one or more other administrative posts carry a vice president's title and a rewarding salary. Each of these posts is a logical step toward the chief financial officer's job.

In many companies today, a variety of special financial-service businesses have been added to the usual finance division complex. These might include an insurance company, a credit business, a leasing operation, a data-processing service, a venture capital pool. The chief financial officer, frequently a senior vice president, is an extremely important member of the corporate hierarchy. He or she attends all board meetings, is often an inside director, and is usually one of the top five earners reported in the proxy statement. Along with the CEO, the CFO is the spokesman for the company to analysts, shareholders, and the press. He has a significant voice in strategy, acquisitions, and broad-based probing.

In recognition of this heightened status, a number of companies have been promoting the CFO to the post of vice chairman. This is particularly true in cases where the chairman and CEO and the president and chief operating officer have operating division backgrounds and limited financial or external relations experience, or when the nature of the company and the breadth of its financial services have enhanced the role of the CFO.

THE MARKETING ROUTE

In the case of consumer packaged goods, it is perfectly logical to begin your climb to the presidency by becoming a brand manager and then to successfully execute a series of higher marketing management posts. These are market-oriented, mass-marketing companies, so the top jobs require an experienced comprehension of this vital end of the business.

But what about those thousands of other companies

out there? Is there a shortcut fast-track route to the top for marketing majors?

My standard answer: The best and quickest way is to gain some exposure, albeit brief, through direct sales experience in an operating division and then to move as rapidly as possible into general management.

If your personal circumstances make it difficult to accept the geographical shifting that goes hand in hand with selling, don't give up. There are exceptions to the selling rule in nearly all companies and there are some other acceptable, but less traveled, paths.

In durable-goods companies, the job of product manager is a highly regarded one. Product managers come from the engineering or research labs, from the plants, from line sales, or from staff marketing. In low-tech product situations, some companies will teach MBAs how to become product managers by special training and by on-the-job progress. After a successful experience as a product manager, it is relatively easy to step into a profit center or another advanced management position—and then you are on your way. The trouble is, these are operating division assignments and not necessarily in the same city as the headquarters office, so you may have to make a move or two.

In many companies, the manager of advertising, sales promotion, market research, or sales training has succeeded at one time or another to a higher-level marketing job. I did it myself at American Standard when I moved from being manager of advertising and sales promotion to become general marketing manager in direct competition with field sales managers.

In practically every company today, there is a dire need for sophisticated marketing leadership. With the advent of the computer, we now know much more about our potential and actual customers: which products and markets return the best profits; how much it costs to create sales and to maintain service; and what customer surveys say. With the strong impact of foreign competition both in the U.S. and around the world, there is an urgent need to revise old marketing thinking and to explore new approaches. With the skilled use of television, teleconferencing, computer graphics, new meeting techniques, and high-speed communications, new ways of selling are rapidly emerging. With the economic necessity to reduce inventory costs, the old channels of distribution, the old methods of transportation, and the old ways of financing sales are giving way to new, creative marketing techniques.

This is where the marketing-minded MBA comes into his or her own. Good companies are finding out how to bring them into their companies, teaching them rapidly about their basic products and seminars, and then putting them to work in useful and exciting jobs. A marketing background is a superb qualification for top executive status. And it's a great place for MBAs to start.

THE CONTROL ROUTE

Not too long ago, controller jobs were thought of as dull, dreary, and dead-end. In corporations, the career path often began with assignment to a traveling auditor's job and then through a long series of operating division jobs, peaking out as vice president–controller. Those MBAs who liked accounting preferred to work with public accounting firms such as Price Waterhouse and Arthur Young, seeking their highly paid partnerships.

In corporations today, the control function is much more important. The controller is the focal point for planning and for reviewing actual performance versus plan over the entire scope of the company. The controller is responsible for seeing that all operations adhere to internal procedures and external requirements. He or she supervises the preparation and issuance of up-to-the-minute complex reports and computerized records, and is an active and influential participant in the budget process, in capital-project authorizations, and critical policy decisions.

In most corporate operating divisions, the controller is one of three candidates to become president of the division—the heads of marketing and operations are the other two. The controller has an equal crack at the job in most companies because of his or her unique perspective, exposure, and involvement in the total work of the division. The division controller also has the opportunity to succeed to the post of vice president–controller of the corporation and in turn become a full-fledged succession candidate for senior vice president–finance of the corporation.

The pathway today to these top accounting and finance jobs differs markedly between companies. Most of the time, it is still a long route through several division groups and headquarter slots. Increasingly, however, companies are setting up fast tracks for their MBA control recruits, compressing the experience curve and promoting the brightest and best as fast as they can take on new responsibility.

THE OPERATIONS ROUTE

The vision that MBAs tend to have of an operations career begins with a dirty job in a steel foundry or on an automotive assembly line as assistant foreman—a lot of grease, smoke, and sweat. There are overtones of labor unions, cramped plant offices, messy factory towns, and menial, unrewarding work. A degree in mechanical, electrical, or chemical engineering is essential. An MBA degree is not.

I guess this still goes on in a few old-fashioned companies, but there are more cases where this career has changed with the times and where MBA skills are brought into play as part of the corporate scheme.

Since service industries now occupy more than half our gross national product, these days the operations jobs are not always in the plants. Instead they tend to be in office buildings in diverse locations, they deal with handling paper and programs rather than the manufacture of products, and they require much less of an engineering approach. The computer and other equipment lend speed and accuracy to quantitative analysis and productivity studies.

As such, the budding young operations executive of the future may deal with the establishment of restaurant or motel franchises; with the institution or operations of software systems for handling credit card vouchers, sales slips, mail order cards, or canceled checks; with production planning and scheduling reports. In a mass-merchandising, mass-item business, the operations function is important, even vital, to the success of the whole program. The operations manager is therefore in the mainstream of the business and has a logical pathway to the topmost executive positions of the company.

In the last few years, more MBAs have been showing more interest in operations careers. They have been taking more operating-related courses and interviewing more actively for operating-type entry jobs.

THE HUMAN RESOURCES ROUTE

Five years ago, I wouldn't have listed this as a separate route for discussion. Very few of our top corporate executives made it through the personnel, industrial relations, or human resources routes.

But times are changing. The part of the corporate equation that deals with people is becoming more important and senior jobs in this area are becoming more significant. Senior human resources executives increasingly report directly to the chairman or president and are called on to participate in major policy decision-making meetings.

There are some companies where the human resources function is extremely important—I am thinking of those with high people-to-cost ratios and those where there has been a history of labor strife, executive turnover, and other problems. In these companies, a tour of duty in the human resources department can be a useful contribution to a career path.

No matter what company you work for, it is necessary to become thoroughly knowledgeable in all facets of human resources administration—governmental, compliance, training and management development, organizational communication, employee benefit administration, and so on.

Don't underestimate the importance of human resources. It still ranks as a staff function in most companies, and as such has not yet become a prime area for launching CEO careers. But it's on its way.

THE PLANNING ROUTE

MBAs are usually good at planning. They feel comfortable and competitive in the strategic planning department of a corporation. They find corporate development work exciting since it deals with mergers and acquisitions and relates closely to the stimulation of investment banking

work. They like the idea of going into "in-house consulting" departments for the same reason.

I'm not much for these jobs for MBAs coming straight
out of business schools. They are very "staffy" jobs and
offer little experience in managing people, developing
leadership skills, or learning about the guts of a business.
It is difficult to be transferred into line, mainstream, decision-making, or other result-measurable jobs.

However, there are four "howevers" here.

1. One is that these planning positions are excellent way
stations for fast trackers. They give an unmatched overall
view of the company at an early stage. *However*, I think it
is advisable to have spent some time first in a line job in
an operating division. The MBA who has a product- and
market-knowledge base is politically more acceptable to
both executives and peers.

2. Second, the planning departments in some companies
today have been so integrated into the functional operation
of the company that they are becoming an acceptable career path. In the large oil corporations, for example, planning is operational in nature and integrated into the whole
plan; at Mobil, former chairman Rawleigh Warner and
former president William Tavoulareas both earned their
managerial spurs in the Mobil planning department. *However*, only a few companies have integrated planning departments this fully, so look well before you leap. Find out
where your second step can logically take you.

3. Third, there *are* some companies who have worked out
a special career track for their MBAs and who specify that
it begin in a staff planning job. Don't fight their system,
but do ask for examples of career path steps followed by
MBAs who have preceded you and, if possible, talk to a

couple of them. If it has worked out well for others, it can do the same for you.

4. The fourth "however" is for the exceptionally talented and lucky MBA who went into an entry staff job, performed well, got transferred into a line responsibility, and lived happily ever after on the fast corporate track.

I remember too clearly my experience fresh out of Harvard Business School. I went to work in the market research department of U.S. Steel. Although it was a rich intellectual experience, I did not go back to U.S. Steel after serving in the navy because I wanted to avoid being typed as a market researcher or a headquarters staffer.

It *is* possible to take the corporate staff route successfully. But I don't recommend it.

SPECIAL ROUTES

Don't let me confine your corporate-career thinking to the routes I have listed above. You can begin with data processing, purchasing, traffic, or a variety of other special staff areas and ultimately find your way out to the promotional mainstream. You might run across a unique starting point with an in-house "intrapreneurial" project, a new product or market team, or an experimental group of some type. You could start overseas in the international section, learn the business, and come back to the U.S. as a maturing, on-the-march executive. You may run into an administrative assistant post or system that works out beautifully for you and for the company.

One of the great things about American business is that there are no sure answers to anything and no guaranteed routes to success. Some of the most interesting young people and senior executives I know are those who break old molds and blaze new trails.

DO IT MY WAY

The most recent survey I have seen of management succession plans at large companies shows that about two-thirds of the eight hundred chief executive officers surveyed predict that their successor will be someone within their company who has come up through the operating divisions. Whether a similar percentage will hold for ten or twenty years more is an open question but the odds are favorable that it will.

But things will not be the same as they were ten or twenty years ago, nor as they are now. And there are a number of conflicting trends that contribute to the confusion. Here are some of them:

• As the annual flood of sixty thousand and more MBAs pours out of the business schools, an increasing number of them will seek careers with industrial corporations, and they will take whatever entry jobs are offered to them.

• As more corporations become accustomed to hiring and handling MBAs, they will develop more and different routes for them to follow.

• As more qualified MBAs begin to compete with one another on the same tracks, corporations will be less willing to pay special premiums and give special attention to these groups—not greatly different than their attitude toward those holding college degrees a couple of decades ago.

• The talents required for tomorrow's managers are getting broader and more sophisticated. The needs for quantitative analysis, financial expertise, planning ability, and communications skills will produce more specialists in such fields.

- There will be a continuous shortage of managers who are capable of doing it all—leading, problem solving, decision making, working with people, troubleshooting, handling public relations, and competing on an internal and external basis.
- There will be an increasing sort-out of the brightest and best educated MBAs. The brightest and best companies will continue to recruit them aggressively and continue to find ways for them to be specially supervised and appraised.
- There will be a continuous shortage of MBAs who are willing to take the difficult route that leads through operating division jobs and which involves a certain amount of geographic transferring to gain specific experience.

The operating division route is not for everyone. It is not an easy road and it has no guarantees that those who take it will reach a presidential destination.

The route exists right now and it will continue to exist for a long time to come. I just wish more of our potential MBA stars would give it a run.

NOT-FOR-PROFIT CAREERS

It may be surprising to those people who think that MBAs are overwhelmingly infatuated with making money to find that a sizable proportion (at Columbia Business School, about 10 percent) of MBAs prefer a career with a not-for-profit institution. This may mean an art museum, a foundation, a charitable organization, an educational institution (both teaching and administrative), the government, a research group, and so forth. Although there are a few highly paid posts in top positions in these fields, most of the jobs pay less than comparable positions in the profit-seeking business world. Why do they choose this path?

The answer that most students give me is, "Because it gives me job satisfaction, and I feel that I am making a contribution. I will get paid enough to live decently. I may end up happier than lots of my classmates."

This is a valid philosophy, and I am delighted to see it, but it takes hard work to find an effective job in this part of the world, too—maybe even more so than in the profit sector. The not-for-profit world is not as well defined or as well organized as the world of profit. They normally don't send recruiters to business schools and they don't have established career paths. Not-for-profit institutions must be sought out and, in some cases, persuaded to hire an MBA. It requires individual initiative and field solicitation of a special kind.

Frequently, the MBAs who seek not-for-profit careers have a special reason. They may be artistically inclined and wish to be associated with various forms of the fine arts; their MBA gives them a chance to do so. They may be politically oriented and wish to begin a governmental career. They may simply be altruistic people who want to utilize their MBA for enhancing their ability to contribute something positive.

Not long ago I received a letter from one of our graduates who said, "I have decided to become an economics teacher in high school. My friends who work for large companies and make good salaries think I am crazy not to enter the job market. They say that I am wasting my MBA and my analytical and communicative skills. I don't think I am because I'm going to be doing something that I like to do and my students will benefit from what I have learned at Columbia Business School. To me this is more important than a career and money. Do you think I am crazy?"

My answer to him was, "I have always admired our graduates who have determined what they wanted to do and have then set forth to do it with vigor and determination. What you are doing is commendable and I congratulate you. On the other hand, after some time, you may wish to reconsider your career path and switch to something that will give you an additional experience, so always keep your options open."

So I say, "Why not?" After all, I moved into a not-for-profit job at Columbia Business School myself. The problem is I waited until I was sixty to do so. If I had known it was going to be so rewarding and so much fun, I might have done it earlier.

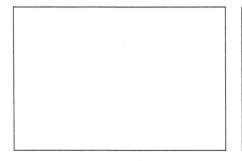

THOSE
FABULOUS
STARTING
SALARIES

Companies are willing to pay those fabulous salaries to newly graduated MBAs for one of two reasons.

1. First, they expect to put the MBA to work immediately in a job where problem-solving, report-writing, and presentation-making skills begin to pay off right away.

This usually means working as a financial analyst, doing strategic planning, becoming an administrative assistant, or performing some type of staff consulting work. These project types of jobs can stand a high turnover rate and it is cheaper to hire a bright, young MBA than it is to engage an outside consultant.

MBAs tend to like these jobs, not only because they feel comfortable within the skill framework, but also because they are often associated with and privy to high-level executives and programs.

For the most part, I don't like to see MBAs take jobs like these. After a while (often three or four years at the most), the MBA begins to realize that he or she is not on a career path, but is in a static, highly paid staff post with limited long-term potential. He or she has not learned a useful "trade," and may well have contributed a great deal to the employer, who got value; but the MBA hasn't really gone anywhere.

The MBA in such a spot must ask, "Now where do I go from here?" and with some frustration, find that the best answer may be to start all over again.

2. In contrast, the second basic reason why companies compete to hire expensive MBAs is that they want to inject them into the long-term management-development processes of their organizations.

MBA recruiters at top companies tell me they have a lot of respect for the selection processes of the leading graduate business schools. The schools accept only those applicants who have demonstrated their intelligence through college courses and aptitude tests. They will have completed an intense graduate curriculum. They have had productive extracurricular activities. They usually have had from two to five years of previous work experience with fine references. It is almost a self-fulfilling prophecy that most of these highly selected people are going to have successful careers—providing they do not box themselves in with inept job selection.

I like to see MBAs go with companies who want them to become long-term candidates for their topmost executive positions. This means, usually, that the company wants the MBA to undertake some specialized product or market training, to be exposed to a variety of working situations and levels, to be fire-tested as to managerial talents. The company is willing to make an investment like this in high-potential MBAs because of the belief that they will be ready to fill critical managerial positions more effectively and sooner than college graduate hirees. As such, the company has a formal or informal fast track for its MBAs and a performance review program to chart their progress.

How do you know if the company you are talking to wants you for a fast-in, fast-out contribution, or whether they seriously want you for the long pull? This is one of the areas for you to ask questions about: to see what has happened to other MBAs in the past few years, to pry out specific examples of successful absorption into the management ranks.

Don't be afraid to discuss this subject with your potential hirers. After all, you are making a commitment of major proportion to them and they should make a similar commitment to you. It is possible, if either of you find yourself distressingly incompatible, to dissolve the arrangement. In so doing, however, you have each lost time and probably money. How much more rewarding it is to do it right the first time!

Inter-
viewing

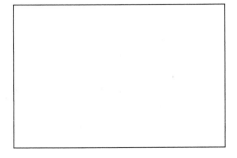

PREPARING
FOR
THE
INTERVIEW

The best way to bust an interview is to prepare for it routinely. Read the material offered. Look through the annual report. Memorize the interviewer's name. Put on your sincere, dark blue uniform. And give them a big smile and a firm handshake.

If the recruiter talks to twenty-five MBAs, that kind of preparation will do no more than get you into one of the twenty runner-up slots.

Of the five people chosen for callbacks at the company, two or three will be those fortunate early draft choices who come equipped with the grades, work experience, and interpersonal skills that were exactly what the recruiter hoped to find. There aren't many of that kind around.

The other two or three who get callbacks, and who have a real crack at the job offer, are those who did something extra, or different, or better.

For example, I urge students, whenever possible, to make a personal visit to the most important local (or nearby) activity of the company *before the interview.* The headquarters office is the best. A plant is excellent. Even the district office of an operating division is good. The people there will be happy to talk to you about their company and will supply you with unusually effective ammunition for your interview, such as information about new products, promotional campaigns, organizational strategies, and other inside information that will demonstrate your interest in and knowledge of the company.

If you are interviewing within a particular industry or field—say, telecommunications, energy, or pharmaceuticals —go get some financial-analyst reports on the industry and the leading players. Read some trade magazines. Look up the *Business Week/Forbes/Fortune* indeces for recent articles. Come up with good, fact-based questions to ask the recruiter. Remember that the interview is a two-way street: you are expected to interview the recruiter as much as he or she interviews you.

Go shopping for the company's product. Talk to an alumnus or friend who works for the company.

You obviously can't do something like this is you're going to have twenty-five eclectic interviews. But you should pull out all the stops on your preferred targets.

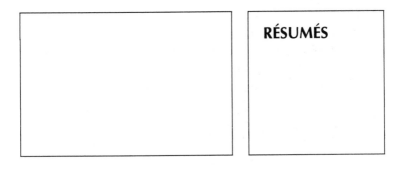

RÉSUMÉS

For Better Résumés

Most business schools have developed a way to teach their MBAs how to write a résumé and there are a number of good books on the subject. It should be easy to follow their directions, but I constantly run across résumés that are carelessly or misguidedly produced. Here are some of the things that turn me off when I read a résumé:

- A typographical error or a misspelling. Why should I hire you if you can't even bother to proofread your own résumé?
- A lie, a half-truth, an exaggeration, an omission. If you bummed around Europe for a year, or played in a rock band for two years, don't try to cover it up. Better to tell the correct story now and capitalize upon the experience.
- A sloppy graphics job. Your résumé doesn't need to be set in type and printed on papyrus. It should, however, be neat, centered, properly spaced, and clean.
- Out-of-date material. Last year's résumé, without your summer job record, tells me that you are lazy, inefficient, or unthinking. It costs so little to keep your per-

sonal record current that you are foolish not to do so.
(This is a good tip to carry with you all during your
business life—you never know when someone might
find it timely to read your résumé.)

- Puffery. It's all right to list your past triumphs as long
as they are meaningful to a prospective employer and
portray pertinent character traits. Let the facts speak
for themselves and don't brag. A little modesty here
may provoke some good responses from an interviewer. It may have been a big deal to be entertainment
chairman at your college fraternity or sorority, but it
isn't going to influence me positively when I interview
you for a job at my corporation.

- Confused objective. This is a tough problem for an
MBA who has a double concentration or who wants to
interview for different types of jobs. I hate to see a
résumé with a job objective that says, "Investment banking, packaged goods manufacturing, or management
consulting." It becomes all but impossible to focus the
personal data you show below properly on any one of
these fields. If it can be so managed, and this is sometimes possible, I much prefer to see a separate résumé
written for each separate job objective. My overall preference, as discussed elsewhere, is to make an all-out
assault on one particular job area, and thus eliminate
this problem. <u>Recruiters are naturally partial to MBAs
who appear to be dedicated to a career in *their* field;</u>
your résumé should reinforce your posture and encourage the recruiter to ask positive questions about
your long-term career objectives.

Don't be alarmed if your MBA-résumé-writing experience is frustrating. It is not an easy task to condense your

life story to a single page and at the same time present yourself to a stranger as a sincere, progressive person with great potential. The several hours you spend in developing a "perfect" résumé will be well worth the time. The Columbia Placement Office provides good hard advice on how to prepare the best résumé you can, so I've included their instructions below and I urge you to read them, as well as the chapter on cover letters that follows.

Résumés

Your résumé is *you* on paper. It is the first picture of you and what you can do, that a potential employer sees. The résumé must sell you! What you have achieved and accomplished in the past is an indication of what you will do in the future; therefore, your résumé must accurately illustrate what you have accomplished, in school and at work. It should be concise, logically ordered, and easily read.

KNOW THE MARKET

The best résumés are written by people who know their market. In general terms, recruiters are looking for potential, as evidenced by excellence, leadership, competitiveness, initiative, human relations (social, persuasive, supervisory), problem solving, oral and written skills, and management skills (organization, coordination, motivation). Different jobs put different emphases on these skills. Know what skills are important in the job you want and slant your résumé accordingly. The more experience you have, the easier it is to slant it to the job. If you don't know the skills emphasized in the job you seek, find out. Talk to the Alumni Counseling Board, a member of the placement staff, professors, or someone you know who has the job now.

KNOW THE PRODUCT—YOU

You know the skills and criteria for the job you want. What experiences in your background illustrate these? First list everything you have done, then select the best or most appropriate items.

In bringing one's job hunt to a successful conclusion one must employ many of the same elements that are utilized successfully in selling a product in the open and *competitive* marketplace. In the case of MBA job applicants, the product they are selling is their ability to perform successfully in the initial job *and* their potential, in the longer run, to assume managerial responsibility.

Thus, it is imperative that you develop a marketing plan to bring your employment efforts to a successful conclusion.

Broadly, the major steps in any marketing campaign are:

1. To analyze and research the product and its applications.
2. To research the marketplace and determine where the product may be effectively and profitably used.
3. To determine the channels best used to get the product in the hands of the consumers in the marketplace.

It is the first of these steps that we wish to expand on here.

Knowing and understanding the product—*your* ability and long-range potential—is the first step of your job campaign and of paramount importance. It is, by no means, a cursory step. This product analysis, or self-assessment as in this case, should be done methodically, thoroughly, and be written out and organized. It will *not* suffice merely to sit down and think briefly about this subject. As you list attributes and other qualities in your analysis, list also examples that illustrate them. Recruiters expect concrete evidence of what you are telling them.

Following is a suggested table that should help you organize your thinking and stimulate your thought processes on the subject. While comprehensive, no such list can ever be complete. Feel free to add or change the categories and subcategories to suit your individual needs.

SELF-ASSESSMENT/SELF-ANALYSIS

Strengths
High energy level.
Initiative.
Intelligence.
Sense of perspective.
Ability to work under
pressure.

Weaknesses
Tendency to procrastinate.
Failure to follow through.
Impatience with detail.

**Accomplishments
and Achievements**
Scholarships.
Success on the job.
Elective or appointive
office held.
Successful competitions.
Life-style.

Decisions You Have Made
(Career, Family, Personal)
Why undergrad school and
major.
Why certain extracurricular
activities.
Why first job.
Why MBA school and
major.
Why this career field.
Why the companies you
are interviewing.
Why the job for which you
are interviewing.
Why your life-style.

Interests
Competitive activities.
Intellectual activities.
People.

Desires
Money.
Power.
Success.
Respect.

Strong Subjects in School
Quantitative.
Conceptual.
Humanistic.
Individual courses.

Weak Subjects
(Same as above.)

Abilities
Communicative ability.
Quantitative ability.
Leadership.
Conceptual ability.
Analytical ability.

Attitudes
Creativity.
Interpersonal skills.
Quantitative.
Conceptual analytical ability.
Ability to set priorities.

Life-style
Location.
Travel.
Commitment to family.

Disappointments Encountered
Job related.
Academic related.
Personal.

Short-Term Goals
In first job.
In development of work-related skills.

Long-Term Goals (5–10 Year)
Power.
Prestige.
Position.
Running things.

Things You Enjoy
Accomplishment.
Competition.
Interpersonal.

Things You Dislike
Personalities.
Tasks.
Environments.
Types of work structure.

Values
Moral.
Personal.
Business.

Relocation	**Travel**
Personal restrictions.	Objections to.
Family restrictions.	Frequency.
Short- and long-term	Desire for.
restrictions.	Tolerance level.
Needs and Restrictions	**Types of People You Like**
Geographical.	**and Dislike**
Ego.	As friends.
Financial.	As business associates.
Health.	As prospective clients and
Social status.	customers.
	As superiors, peers, subordinates.
	Spouse's Plans and Career Goals
	Dual-career family?
	Children?
	Short and long term.

Remember, this is meant to be your guide in helping you to understand and to *sell* your ability and potential in the MBA job market. After completing your self-analysis, go over each listing and ask yourself: "Why did I include this?" Delve into the background—depth in understanding your product is just as important as breadth. Recruiters will be interested in more than just surface exposure. "Why?" or "Why did you say this?" or "Why do you feel this way?" are just the sort of questions they will ask when probing into your background.

The weaknesses side of the coin is just as important for you to be aware of as the strengths side. Interviewers may perceive them or ask you what they are directly. You must know how to handle this kind of questioning—just as any good salesperson would—and redirect the questioning or turn the suspected product weakness into a sales strength.

Most interviewers, regardless of the job they are seeking to fill or the industry they represent, are looking for certain attributes that indicate potential—intelligence, leadership, motivation, competitiveness, ambition, initiative, common sense, energy, enthusiasm, and direction, to name some of the more obvious. They are also looking for skills—interpersonal, quantitative, conceptual, analytical, organizational, and communicative come to mind immediately. The emphasis they place on each, and the order in which they would rank them, will depend on job content, industry, organization style and structure, and other factors. Thus, after doing your "product analysis," you should begin to design it to sell with the "buyer needs" in mind.

Keep firmly in mind that the results of this self-analysis *must* be like a product analysis. They must be realistic and give you a basis for going into the job market with sufficient background knowledge to sell yourself to prospective employers. Be honest with and true to yourself. Don't try to become someone you are not, but *do not* sell yourself short.

Keep in mind, too, as you enter the MBA job market, that you are not the only one doing so. There is a great deal of *intense* competition out there. Evaluate your competitive position realistically.

ORGANIZATION

If you have limited work experience, your primary background has been school; so begin with academic achievements. Possible areas of experience are offices held, athletics, drama, music, debate, internships, special study or research, self-started businesses, active club memberships, community activities, volunteer experiences, part-time jobs. Focus on what you have initiated, were responsible for, and achieved.

If you have considerable work experience, college activities will be less important, with the exception of business school and academic achievements and honors. List your jobs, writing out your responsibilities and achievements. Then review your market and slant your résumé appropriately. Highlight the skills most attractive to your market. For example, if your experience is heavily quantitative and you are applying for a people-contact job, you may want to emphasize your people-contact skills and downplay the quantitative skills. Leave out unimportant duties.

WORDING

The key to an effective résumé is clear, concise, simple language. Condense, trim, clarify. Recruiters don't have unlimited time to read résumés. Help them in this task. The pertinent facts and skills should stand out at a glance, and not be buried in verbose, murky descriptions.

Sentences or phrases should be short, ten words maximum, beginning with a capital letter. Leave out descriptions of the company or product and the articles "a," "the," "an." Avoid weak phrases like "was responsible for," "duties included," "assisted in," "worked on." You are not writing a job description. Focus on action. *What you did rather than what you were.* Stress results by giving concrete examples of what you did.

1. For a dynamic impact, start with action words such as
2. "managed," "controlled," or "administered." Don't use the same word twice in one paragraph unless you have a reason
3. for emphasizing it. Quantify whenever possible: number of people, number of items, amount of money involved,

amount of time saved. Use numbers or percentages. Don't write out "ten"; use numerals: "10." If you are changing careers, it helps to use the vocabulary of business to describe your nonbusiness experience.

 Write and rewrite your experiences, trimming your wording until it projects, in as few words as possible, the sharp, clear image of you as an achiever. Review the résumé with others.

FORMAT

For the résumé book, use the William Cole format: Professional Objective, Education, Experience, and Additional Information, with dates in the left margin. Recruiters have requested this standard format: it makes the résumé book more professional and easier for them to use. Your résumé *must* be one page for the résumé book (this is a bound book of graduating students' résumés that most business schools make available to recruiting companies). It *should* be one page for other purposes as well. Since recruiters don't have much time to read résumés, they appreciate a concise presentation and may not read a second page anyway.

For résumés you send out, or hand in for each on-campus interview, you should alter the format to emphasize your strong selling points, perhaps switching the education and experience sections. On-campus recruiters are more comfortable with a specific job objective. This means you may have more than one résumé.

Your résumé should be typed on a professional typewriter (e.g., IBM Executive, not on your home portable), and preferably with a carbon ribbon. Proofread it carefully! It should be offset or photocopied on good quality paper. If you are using a professional service, be sure to see a sample of their work first. Demand perfection. Keep the format of your résumé open. Use blank space effectively to invite reading. Don't pack the page with print. Use underlining and caps to emphasize the important items. For example, if you are changing careers, you won't underline your previous titles—that would only emphasize the career change. If you had several minor jobs in a short period of time, you may want to leave one out, or condense them into one short phrase. To help camouflage short periods of unemployment, indicate year(s) only ("1975"), rather than months and year(s) ("5/75 to 10/75"). Do not abbreviate words.

NAME

Do not use nicknames. Place your name in the upper right corner or in the center. The left corner gets stapled to other papers and your name is lost.

ADDRESS

Under name, or on the right, indicate a current address where you can be reached. If necessary, indicate on the left an alternate address and the date it will become effective.

PHONE NUMBER

Be sure to include area code. Give your home phone number or, if necessary, use a number where messages can be left for you during the day.

PROFESSIONAL OBJECTIVE

Prospective employers tend to be more comfortable with a job objective. *It is required* for the résumé book. Do not say "desire to apply my education and experience to a challenging growth position in _____." All that is assumed. Indicate the area in which you want to work; make it general, e.g., commercial banking. Indicate your functional area of interest, e.g., corporate finance. Check old résumé books for other examples.

For on-campus interviews, tailor your objective to the position. Be as specific as possible. Check the worklists handed out each week for descriptions. Paraphrase if possible.

For answering an advertisement, paraphrase the job description given in the ad. For a mass mailing, *omit* objective completely on the résumé, but describe it in your cover letter.

For a summer job application, make clear that your objective is "Summer position in _____," so you are not confused with a full-time applicant.

EDUCATION

Give name(s) of college(s) and graduate school(s) where a degree or pertinent certificate was granted, most recent first, then in reverse chronological order. Street address is not necessary; city and state is optional. For dates use the years only. If you dropped out and then returned, making an awkward listing of years, use graduation year only. *But:* be sure to indicate *month* and *year* of business school graduation.

Indicate degree awarded, concentration or major, honors and awards. Undergraduate memberships and offices are optional; they are less important for those with several years of work experience.

Tuition financing. Jobs can be listed here or under

experience, depending on emphasis. Other financing, e.g., loans, scholarships, savings, may also be listed—again, this is more important for those with limited work experience.

EXPERIENCE

Describe position held, most recent first, then in reverse chronological order. For dates use years only. Give employer's name, city, and state. Street address is not necessary. Give your title. If you didn't have one, make up a sensible, realistic approximation. For summer jobs, "intern" or "trainee" is perfectly acceptable. For suggestions about describing what you did, re-read the "Wording" section above. It is not necessary to indicate part-time or volunteer work.

ADDITIONAL INFORMATION

1. Include relevant special skills (computer programming, computer languages) and relevant certifications (CPA). If
2. you know any foreign languages, use a separate section and indicate level of expertise (fluent in, working knowledge of, familiar with).

Publications and papers you have presented may be included in the education section or in a separate section depending on the emphasis you want. Hobbies, special interests, and foreign travel can serve as useful ice-breakers and as a common, nonwork, meeting ground between you and the interviewer. But they are optional.

Citizenship (for foreign nationals)—if you have a Permanent Residence Visa (PRV), put it in your résumé. If not, leave citizenship off, unless you wish to return to your country.

Do not include personal data such as height, weight, age, marital status, or health.

Here are a few sample résumés:

EXAMPLE A

ELSIE COLE
435 West 119th Street, #2E
New York, NY 10027
(212) 666-1234
(212) 280-8220 messages

PROFESSIONAL OBJECTIVE

Position in Marketing*

EDUCATION

1985–1987 **COLUMBIA UNIVERSITY GRADUATE SCHOOL OF BUSINESS**
MBA—Marketing—May 1987
Beta Gamma Sigma. Dean's List. Vice President, Women in Business. Member, American Marketing Association. Business manager, The Bottom Line; increased advertising revenue by 20%. Financed education through part-time employment.

1977–1981 **UNIVERSITY OF MICHIGAN**
BA—Economics—June 1981
Dean's List. Student Council Representative. Vice President, Economic Society. Varsity volleyball, 3 years. Financed education through loans and summer work as bank clerk, bookkeeper, and retail salesperson.

*If appropriate, this may read: Summer position in Marketing.

EXPERIENCE

Summer 1986   **ABC COMPANY,** New York, New York
Assistant Product Manager/Frozen Foods Division—Assisted in initial phases of new product introduction, including marketing research and sales promotion. Recommended pricing strategy which was implemented. Product currently in test markets.

1982–1985   **XYZ COMPANY,** Seattle, Washington
Regional Sales Manager/Restaurant Supplies Division—Responsible for sales in Seattle-Tacoma region. Supervised 2 sales representatives. Increased number of clients by 15% and gross sales by 30%. Average annual sales in excess of $2,000,000. Wrote procedures manual as training aid which was adopted company-wide.

1981–1982   **Sales Representative**—Completed training program. Assigned territory in Seattle-Tacoma region. Sold 120% of quota during first year. Promoted to Regional Sales Manager ahead of schedule.

ADDITIONAL INFORMATION   Fluent in Spanish. Traveled extensively in Mexico. Enjoy bridge, public speaking, and scuba diving. Active member, University of Michigan Alumni Association.

EXAMPLE B

EDWARD COLE

20 Washington Avenue   435 West 119th Street #2E
Fort Worth, TX   New York, NY 10027
                                              (212) 666-4321
                                              (212) 280-8220 messages

**PROFESSIONAL
OBJECTIVE**

Position in Finance.*

EDUCATION

1985–1988   **COLUMBIA UNIVERSITY GRADUATE
                SCHOOL OF BUSINESS
                COLUMBIA UNIVERSITY SCHOOL OF INTER-
                NATIONAL AND PUBLIC AFFAIRS**
                MBA/MIA—Joint Degree Candidate—
                August 1988
                Dean's List, Columbia Business School.
                Member, American Finance and Interna-
                tional Banking & Finance Associations.
                Graduate Research Assistant, Middle East
                Institute.

1978–1982   **UNIVERSITY OF MICHIGAN**
                BA—History—May 1982
                Cum Laude, College Scholar, Dean's List.
                Member, Varsity Tennis Team. Wesleyan
                Program in Paris, Fall.

EXPERIENCE

Spring 1986   **LMN COMPANY**   New York, New York
                **Assistant Product Manager/Frozen Foods
                Division**—Assisted in initial phases of new
                product introduction, including marketing
                research and sales promotion. Recom-
                mended pricing strategy which was imple-
                mented. Product currently in test markets.

*If appropriate, this may read: Summer position in Finance.

1983–1985	**QRW BANK** Boston, Massachusetts **Senior Money Market Trader**—Traded government securities and money market instruments. Analyzed interest rate swaps and mortgaged backed securities. Coordinated interest sensitive analyses. Adapted software programs for IBM PC.
Summers 1978–1982	**GLWN COMPANY** Boston, Massachusetts **Partner/Owner**—Developed entrepreneurial venture in the maintenance of privately owned clay and grass tennis courts. Employed 30 college students annually. Sold share of business for $20,000
ADDITIONAL **INFORMATION**	Traveled independently throughout Western Europe, Summer and Fall 1982. NASD Registered. Active alumnus of Phillips Andover.

EXAMPLE C

EVELYN COLE
2 MacDougal Street
New York, NY 10012
(212) 222-4444

PROFESSIONAL **OBJECTIVE**	Summer position in Non Profit Management.
EDUCATION 1985–1987	**COLUMBIA UNIVERSITY GRADUATE** **SCHOOL OF BUSINESS** MBA—Public Non Profit Management— May 1987

1975–1979   **BARNARD COLLEGE**
BA—English—May 1979
Phi Beta Kappa. President and founder,
Victorian Society.
Member and performer, Gilbert and Sulli-
van Society.

1971–1975   **BRONX HIGH SCHOOL OF SCIENCE**
National Merit Finalist.

EXPERIENCE

1979–1984   **N.E.W. THEATER COMPANY,** New York, New
York

A.C.T. EXPERIMENTAL THEATER, New York,
New York

G.E.M. PRODUCTION, Tanglewood, Massachusetts

S.U.N. PRODUCTION, Jacob's Pillow, New
York
Actress—Performed principal and support
roles for Off-Broadway and summer stock
productions. Member of Actors Equity.
Cited as "Brightest New Face on Off-
Broadway this Season" (1983) by Theater
Review critic John Swift.

Summer 1978   **DISTRICT 12 PUBLIC SCHOOLS,** New York,
New York
Volunteer—Taught English to non-English
speaking adults.
Pilot Program in adult education subse-
quently adopted throughout New York
State.

ADDITIONAL
INFORMATION   Fluent in Spanish. Traveled extensively
throughout Spain and Portugal. Enjoy ten-
nis, swimming, and classical music. President,
2 MacDougal Street Tenants Association.

THE COVER LETTER

The cover letter (sometimes known as the letter of transmittal, letter of application, or Letter of Introduction) is a valuable—often crucial—part of your total job-hunting campaign. This letter, along with your résumé, serves to introduce you to a potential employer and to develop sufficient interest in you to warrant a personal interview.

The letter should be short and to the point, designed to be read by a person with limited time. While every letter should be a creative effort and individually written, there are generally accepted standard features of the common cover letter.

FIRST PARAGRAPH. This is a quick introduction: who you are; why you are writing; how you heard of the opening; what position you seek; who suggested you write; what it is about the organization that is motivating you to write. You may wish, in this opening paragraph, to mention that you will be or are an MBA.

SECOND PARAGRAPH. Referring to your work and/or academic background, demonstrate why you are both interested and qualified for the position, the organization, or the field. Try not to simply repeat the résumé, but to amplify on the *achievement* aspects of your background—briefly! It is better to highlight how well you did something, rather than just mention what you did—quantify if possible. This may be the opportunity to "update" the résumé with a new bit of activity (extracurricular, grades, etc.).

THIRD PARAGRAPH.   The concluding paragraph contains a reference to the action you wish to see taken. Specifically, you would like to meet with the person to whom you have written in order to discuss your background in a personal interview. You have several options on how to manage this: you can await a written or phoned reply, or you can follow up with a phone call yourself. The cover letter with résumé, followed by a phone call, is most aggressive and direct, and leaves little room for clerical or administrative oversight on the organization's part to interfere with your interview opportunity.

The phone call is particularly appropriate to local organizations, where travel will not be a problem. If you are writing a distant company and planning to be in the area, let them know this. More often than not, an organization will not pick up your expenses merely on the basis of a letter and résumé.

SOME GENERAL CONSIDERATIONS.   Cover letters should always be (or at least look) individually prepared. The letters should be specifically tailored to the organization itself. Specific knowledge of the job requirements is a great help in writing the cover letter. With this knowledge, you can demonstrate exactly how your previous background, experience, or skills can be of value in meeting the requirements of the particular job and company. Of course, some requirements are universal: maturity, intelligence, aggressiveness, imagination, and good interpersonal skills. These can be demonstrated to the prospective employer either experientially (work) or inferentially (academic and extracurricular achievements, interests and hobbies).

DRESS CODE

Most of the time, when I counsel MBAs, I tend to be on the liberal side. I urge them to be creative, do something different, take a calculated risk.

When it comes to dressing for an interview, I'm the worst old fogy in the world. The only way to do it is to

Dress Conservatively!

Men: Wear a conservatively cut dark gray or blue suit, a plain blue or white shirt, and a quiet silk tie. Wear shoes, not loafers, and over-the-calf socks. If you need a coat, wear a lined raincoat or overcoat. Save your linen jacket, fancy handkerchiefs, and leather tie for weekends.

Women: Wear a conservatively cut dark suit or dress with equally restrained accessories. Go light on the makeup and jewelry. Don't get an elaborate hairdo. Wear a cloth coat, not fur. Save your slit skirts and gauzy blouses for parties.

Why so stodgy and dull? Because the interviewer should concentrate on you. Don't let a sartorial aberration distract him or her from what you have to say. Let your entrepreneurial spirit show through in your résumé, not in your mode of dress.

I'm not forcing you into a uniform straitjacket. It is

prudent and wise to invest in some reasonably expensive clothes for your interviews—you probably need only one full set—and they will last a long time. Spend time shopping and thinking about your selections; it can make a difference.

I'm equally fussy about grooming. Young men enjoy the privilege of cultivating beards and letting their hair grow while at school. While interviewing, however, clean-shaven is best. Get hired and established; then let it grow again if you wish.

Another thing to take off for the interview is fat. It is unbecoming on most people, because everyone knows that a little dieting, exercise, and willpower makes you look better. Looking trim adds to the impression that you have control of yourself, and, of course, feeling fit and healthy gives you a great competitive edge.

The above comments on dress, grooming, and physical presentation may sound trite, conservative, and obvious, but I note an alarming number of exceptions to these admonitions. I have seen MBAs waiting for their interviews in unshined shoes, with unkempt hair, garish styling, and loud colors shouting all over the place. Why spend all that money on your MBA and then not give your critical interviews your best shot?

TAPE YOURSELF

At your business school, you probably have a videotape machine and an arrangement whereby an MBA can be given a mock interview by a trained student-worker. Most intelligent MBAs avail themselves of this vital service and, without fail, find some personal mannerisms that need to be corrected before the *serious* interviewing begins. These mannerisms run the gamut from nose pulling to mumbling, slumping, or giggling, to seeming pushy, to talking too fast or too much.

To students who use the tape and who try to improve their interviewing techniques, and come back again to tape their new style—congratulations. You have greatly enhanced your chances of having a rewarding interview.

To students who haven't bothered to tape themselves—be aware that you are granting a competitive advantage to your fellow students who vie with you for job offers. And you're missing a chance to gain an advantage over those who didn't bother.

If your school has no videotapes, then find someone who has a video or movie camera, write out an interview and play it back. Get a friend to critique you. You're betting on your career, so you might as well play all the cards.

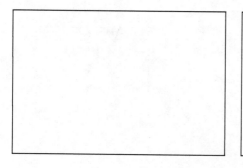

**BE
CREATIVE**

Hundreds of companies use business schools each year to hold recruiting interviews with graduating MBAs. This works out to up to twenty interviews for each person.

These are, for the most part, companies that interview intensively at many business schools; they seek, and usually get, the cream of the country's annual MBA crop. They usually have highly organized fast tracks for their hirees to run on. And each year they put dozens of new MBAs to work. It is a very competitive situation.

It is much too easy for MBAs to confine their interviews to those companies who come to the school and are sponsored by the placement division. This is a shame because there are *several thousand* good companies out there who occasionally hire an MBA or two and who offer excellent career prospects without the overblown competition. Because they do not go out to the business schools, many of them have never hired an MBA or, as I tell my students, are deprived of the privilege of having MBAs contribute to their corporate well-being.

The answer, of course, is for students to exercise their creativity and vigor and go to the company rather than wait patiently for America's great companies to come to them.

**SHOW
THE
REAL
YOU**

Some of the most responsive people to consult with on interviewing techniques are recent alumni who come to their school on MBA recruiting assignments. Their own interviewing experiences are still fresh and they are empathic with the students they see.

I have talked at some length with a number of these observers and this is a summary of what they tell me about the interviewees and about what the interviewers want to see and hear.

- MBAs are much too patterned and predictable in their interviews. They ask the same questions in the same deadly serious way. Little creative thought is applied. Most of the interviewees get lumped together into a dull, monotonous group.
- Personality should be allowed to come through. Recruiters are looking for people who will fit into the culture and the structure of their company. Let them see who you are.
- Don't overanalyze the situation by prejudging what the recruiter wants to hear. Spend less time mouthing platitudes and more on expressing yourself.
- Take a few chances in the interview. If you sense an opening or a sympathetic ear, be prepared to ask a

more aggressive question. Don't be a smart aleck, of course, but try to do something different that will make the recruiter remember you in a favorable way. (Here is a good time to inject some of the special information you have developed from your own personal research on the company. See pages 109–10 for a few ideas.)

- <u>Always give it your best shot.</u> If you show any signs of boredom or a perfunctory response, you are asking for a bullet. Keep your enthusiasm at high intensity throughout the interview.

- Remember that many are called, but very few are chosen. Make it a memorable experience for both of you.

One of my former students, who is now recruiting for the capital markets group of a large bank, says, "Now that I have seen the interview process from the recruiter's side of the table, I wish I could go back and do it all over again. I would be much less stereotyped and would work much harder on getting my personal philosophy across."

RECRUITERS' ADVICE TO JOB-SEEKING STUDENTS

The Columbia Business School Placement Office has compiled this summary of suggestions recruiters believe will make the process more productive for them and for you.

WHAT TURNS ON RECRUITERS AT ON-CAMPUS INTERVIEWS

1. Evidence of self-analysis—you know why you're in the interview.
2. Evidence that you take the interview seriously, as demonstrated by being well prepared for it.
3. Enthusiasm.
4. Recognition that interviewing is a difficult process.

WHAT TURNS OFF RECRUITERS

1. Lack of preparation—evidence of lack of interest.
2. Inappropriate qualifications for positions the firm is seeking to fill, as noted on placement office work lists.
3. Overconfidence, cockiness, put-ons, falseness, superficiality, late arrival for interview.

QUALITIES RECRUITERS LOOK FOR

1. *General:* See your boy/girl scout manual: ambition, poise, sincerity, trustworthiness, articulateness, analytical ability, initiative, interest in the firm. (Overall general intelligence is assumed because you're here, believe it or not.) Different firms look for different kinds of people, different kinds of personality, style, appearance, ability, and technical skill. Always check the posted job specs for any interview, and don't waste time by talking about a job you can't do or for which you don't have the minimum qualifications.

2. *Dress:* Look like a businessperson unless there's a sensible extenuating circumstance—and if there is, *do explain.* Be neat and clean. Don't be sloppy. Don't dress in an extreme way.

3. *Grades:* The importance of grades varies from firm to firm. For some they're critical, for others unimportant. Be sure to check job specs posted. Be able to explain marked deficiencies, if asked. On-campus interviewers don't know your grades in advance but are likely to ask you about them. They *may* ask you to release your transcript. They *may* ask you the name of a faculty reference of *your* choice or they *may* later inquire about you from a faculty member whom *they* know personally.

4. *Experience:* Again, this varies from job to job. Check posted specifications. "Two years experience" means you have to have a *minimum of two years experience!* If you've had work experience, be able to articulate the importance of what you did in terms of the job for which you are interviewing and in terms of your own growth or learning.

5. *Knowledge of the recruiter's company and industry:* At a minimum, you really *are* expected to have read everything the company has put in the placement library. Don't waste interview time asking questions you could have had answered by the printed material. Know the firm's position and character relative to others in the same industry. General awareness of media coverage of a firm and its industry is usually expected.

YOUR RÉSUMÉ—WHAT IT'S USED FOR

1. To provide the interviewer with a set of topics to discuss.

2. To provide the interviewer with a concise picture of the applicant.

3. To present the applicant's major qualification for the job: education (business school major), work experience (and its significance), extracurricular activities.

4. It is usually *not* used as a negative screening device.
5. Remember that you have to be prepared to answer any questions raised by your résumé.

THE OFFICE INTERVIEW

1. Call the day before to confirm the appointment.
2. Be on time.
3. Remember that you want to find out if you really want to work for them.
4. You want to find out what the company is looking for and expects of you if you are hired: overtime, travel, relocation, dress, skills, etc.
5. Remember what points about yourself you want to make.
6. Don't oversell. Be yourself. Relax.

SUMMARY

1. *Be yourself.* You have to figure out who you are (for the time being) and be that person.
2. *Do your homework* about the company and the job.
3. *Take the interview seriously.* If you aren't prepared, don't waste your time or the interviewer's.
4. *Dress appropriately.* Extremes create bad first impressions. Go/no-go decisions are sometimes made *very* early in the interview. First impressions can be critical.
5. *No half-truths or falsehoods anywhere*—interviews, résumé, etc.

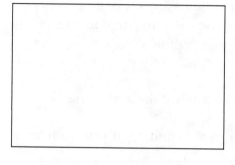

**MAKING
YOUR
INTERVIEW
WORK
FOR
YOU**

It is just as important to ask good questions during the interview as it is to give intelligent answers to the recruiter's questions. You should be prepared to inquire about some topics which are not covered in the literature in order to show your interest in the organization and the knowledge you have already acquired about it as well as interest in your own career prospects and development.

Following are some general topics you can use as a springboard to formulate your own questions. Once again, try to be sure your questions have not been answered in the company literature; otherwise it may appear that you did not do your homework very well. Also be sure to show your inquiries are in proper context within the interview and founded on sincere interest. Trite or idle queries are obnoxious and detrimental to your chances.

Topics You May Want to Cover

THE COMPANY

Strengths, what they are, how management capitalizes on them.

Weaknesses, what they are, how management deals with them.

Changes in the industry, what management expects, steps being taken.

Best opportunities within firm for new MBAs.

Competition, who main competition is.

Long-term strategies contemplated by firm.

Legislation pending which may affect firm—and how.

Major source of business in next few years.

Steps being taken to respond to changing environment.

Organizational/department planning methods.

Generalist or specialist orientation within firm.

TRAINING AND DEVELOPMENT

Formal program, mechanics, length.

General or specialized exposure within the firm.

Opportunities to gain experience in other areas of the firm.

Expectations of the new MBA, importance of previous experience.

Independent work, group, or apprenticeship.

Formal classroom training, on the job, or combination.

Continuing education opportunities

WORK

How assignments are made.

Input individual has into final location or department.

Independent or team structure.

Supervision, number of people to report to, how often.

Deadlines, how often, how much advance notice.

Major support facilities, research department, computer facilities.

Contact between different departments.

Responsibilities and obligations during first year.

Typical career path within company.

Special problems for the MBAs, nature and solutions.
Specialization of work—one type of project or variety.
Department structure, information flows.

CONDITIONS

Travel—amount, length, where.
Hours, overtime, peak periods of year.
Evaluation, formal or informal, by whom, for whom.
Critical variables in evaluation and advancement.
Frequency of advancement, role of seniority.
Statement of "work ethic," philosophy of firm.

PEOPLE

Coworkers—background, age, previous experience.
Number of hires per year.
Work environment—competitive, supportive.
Socializing among coworkers.
Rate of turnover—explanation of why high or low.

In general, show familiarity with current events as they affect the industry and firm. Use a recent edition of *The Readers' Guide to Periodical Literature* to find any articles about the industry or firm which you can use for discussion and questions. However, avoid discussion of sensitive issues unless the recruiter mentions them first. Your intimate knowledge of the problems a firm is experiencing may not always favorably impress the recruiter. Be tactful and accentuate the positive. Don't ask trivial questions just to ask questions. Don't be verbose. *Do* be genuinely interested in knowing the answers to the questions you ask and listen patiently and attentively as they are given. Expand upon the answer to the question if you feel it is appropriate to do so. Questions about salary, benefits, and vacation are more appropriate to ask in a second or third interview after it is determined that there is a substantial level of interest in you as a candidate for the position.

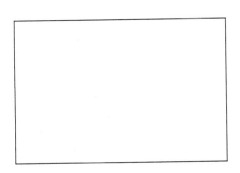

ANTICIPATING QUESTIONS

There are many kinds of interviewers whom MBA job applicants must face: skilled professionals from the college recruitment department; senior personnel officers; practicing executives who have had lots of experience at talking to MBAs, both at schools and during callbacks; executives who are highly experienced in their work, but who are neophytes at MBA interviewing; recent MBA graduates who have been sent back to their schools to screen candidates.

Because of this mix, interview patterns differ sharply. The interviewees who do well in all of these sessions have to be able to deal equally with widely differing interviewing styles.

In some cases, they are expected to listen politely and ask appropriate questions. In others, they may have to react to a confrontational or provocative approach. Prospective employers like to use these pace changes because

it lets them see how the MBAs handle themselves in a
variety of situations.

Despite differing approaches, nearly all interviewers
ask three questions, and it behooves MBAs to be ready to
answer them clearly and succinctly.

1. "Why do you think you would like to work for our
company?"

If you *really* do want a job with that company, then you
should prepare a specific answer that gives good, specific
reasons.

An appropriate answer may go something like this:
"I'm not sure that I do want to work for your company. I
am sure that I want to work in your industry group and
I know that you are one of the leading companies. I have
some questions that I would like to ask *you*" (and then be
prepared with some good ones). You might ask about corporate strategic plans that you have read up on, about
international competitive trends, about management-development programs, or you might ask for examples of
careers within the company that have been rewarding. The
better your homework, the better your questions will be.

The worst answer is one that is flippant, vague, ram-
bling, ill-informed, or negative. You just blew the interview.

2. "If you come with us, what would you expect to be
doing five years or so from now?"

This is an excellent chance for you to discuss the company's career path to a specific job goal—brand manager,
commercial lending officer, project leader, supervising
manager, whatever it is you have in mind.

It is also a good time to ask questions in return as to
what has happened to the MBAs who were hired five years
ago, what training programs are projected, what the *com-*

pany expects to have its MBAs doing in that time, and so forth.

The question is not usually meant to be answered in money, title, or power terms. It is designed to provoke a realistic discussion of values and goals and to see how the company's views fit with those of the MBA.

③ "Looking way down the road, say twenty to twenty-five years, what would you see yourself doing if you came and stayed with our company?"

This is the big pie-in-the-sky question that is designed to stimulate lofty discussion of ideals and ambitions. In some cases, it is a silly and meaningless question, but it should always be answered seriously.

A reasonable answer might be, "At that time I will be about fifty years old. I hope I will have been successful enough as a manager so that I will be one of the senior (marketing, finance, operating) executives in the corporation. I would like to think of myself as a long-term candidate for one of the very top posts, but this also depends upon the future of the company itself. What do you expect will be happening to your company by that time?"

In each of these Q-and-A situations, you should try to keep the discussion moving, to allow for questions to come from both sides and to bring out specific value information that is useful for both the company and you in playing this serious mating game.*

Try to end the interview on a high note. The interviewer, almost invariably, will give you a cue as to its windup. He or she will look at the time, pick up the schedule, stand up, or say something of a farewell nature.

---

*AUTHOR NOTE: Specific value information consists of details from your experiences which lead the interviewer to recognize your special qualities.

Be ready for this. Don't fumble and mumble in a surprised way. Stand up, shake hands, and say in your own words (if you mean it!), "It was a pleasure to have interviewed you and your company. I particularly enjoyed our discussion about (international experience, task-force work, product training, whatever). I look forward, with great interest, to the possibility of a future meeting because I am extremely interested in your company."

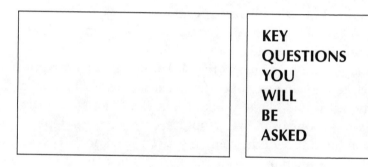

**KEY
QUESTIONS
YOU
WILL
BE
ASKED**

The Columbia Business School Placement Office recently polled students about the questions most frequently asked and those they thought were most difficult in interviews, both here at the school and at company offices. Sharing their answers with you might be helpful in preparing you for the questions you, too, will face. Remember, each interview and interviewer is unique but anticipation of many of the questions can enable you to prepare thoughtful and intelligent answers. These questions cannot, of course, be organized the way they may be asked.

The arrangement here is designed merely for convenient review.

PERSONAL

1. Tell me about yourself. (Be prepared for this question and have your answer ready—for example, a short statement saying where you were born, raised, went to college, leading up to graduate school and why you are taking this interview. Please be imaginative; we don't want all business school students saying the same thing.)
2. How do you keep abreast of current events?
3. How do you relieve everyday tensions?
4. Describe your weaknesses—which is your major weakness? How do you compensate for it? Describe your strengths—which is your greatest asset? Your skills. (Try to show them to best advantage in light of the company or industry you are talking to.)
5. Have you ever failed? What did you learn from it?
6. What do you do when you're weak or deficient in a particular area (statistics, accounting, etc.)? How do you compensate for it?
7. What do you judge your major successes and accomplishments to have been? (How did you achieve these?) Your failures? Your major disappointments? (How did these come about?)
8. What were the three (five) most important events (decisions) of your life? What decisions have you most regretted? Why?
9. In two to five years, when you look back, what would you like to have accomplished?
10. Are you a leader, an entrepreneur, creative? Why do you say you are? (Be prepared to give examples.)

11. How would your friends describe you?

12. Are you more of a team player or an entrepreneur?

13. How important is money to you?

14. What does your spouse do? Do you entertain often at home?

15. How did you like your summer (previous) job? What did you get out of it? What did you learn about yourself? What was the most rewarding thing about this (these) job(s)? Why did you decide to leave it (them)?

16. If you had a chance to do things differently in one of your previous jobs, what would you do?

17. What do you really want to do?

18. What are the attributes of an ideal job for you?

19. What makes you want to be a _____ (position applied for)? Why would you be good at it?

20. What makes you think you could be a success in business?

21. How well do you work independently? With others?

22. If you could change the conditions under which you work, what would you do?

23. How are you doing in your present job search?

24. What do you read?

25. Define cooperation, leadership.

26. How do you define consulting?

27. Who have you talked to today?

28. What other organizations are you talking to?

29. How did you decide on each one?

30. What do you expect to get out of a career?

31. Where do you expect to be in five, ten years? On what do you base this?

32. You have five minutes to describe the most relevant and specific items in your background which show that you are uniquely qualified for this job. (Prepare several

important points; to have the interviewer remember you after you have left, stress them in a short, concise statement.)

33. Think of someone you like/dislike and tell me what makes you like/dislike this person so much.

34. Tell me about your home life when you were growing up. Parents' occupations.

35. Are you tough? Are you aggressive? (Be prepared to back up your answers.)

36. How competitive are you? Will you fight to get ahead?

37. Do you like hard work, routine or challenging work? Why?

> Comment: During your interviewing process you may be asked about your motivation to do various things. The interviewers really want to see the extent of your motivation, and also your character, personality, and leadership potential.

EDUCATION

1. Why did you choose _____ (your undergraduate college or university)?

2. When and why did you major in art, history, etc.? With your background, why didn't you major in _____?

3. If you were planning to go into business, why did you major in history, or _____ at the undergraduate level?

4. When did you first make up your mind that you wanted to go to business school? Why did you make this decision? What schools did you apply to? Why did you pick _____?

5. How are you doing here in school? What courses are you doing best in? The worst in? What have you gotten out of your courses?

6. What courses have you taken in your major field? What electives?
7. What courses have you liked the most? The least?
8. Did your goals change while you were in business school?
9. In school, what did you do with your time?
10. What have you learned at business school that will help you on this job?
11. Tell me about your high school years. Your college years.
12. What prompted you to get an MBA?
13. What makes you a standout among your peers?
14. What do you think about your experiences at _____ _____ (your business school)?
15. Did _____ (your business school) fulfill your expectations?

JOB, COMPANY, INDUSTRY

1. Why are you interested in marketing? Why product management? Why advertising? Why finance? Why commercial banking? Why investment banking? Why corporate treasuryship? Why financial analysis?
2. Why are you interested in this industry? This particular company?
3. Tell my why you think the life-style of this job is right for you.
4. Make a comparison of our firm (industry) and the others you are talking to.
5. Are you interviewing with the company you worked for last summer? Why or why not?
6. What do you think you will be doing in this job you are applying for? What do you think this job requires, and how do you match those requirements? What do you

think the duties of an account executive (or whatever) are? Why do you think you're suited for _____?

7. Do you want to move into line management?
8. Given your background in (a different field), why do you want to become a (marketing manager, etc.)?
9. How do you foresee the future of our industry?
10. From your past work experience, what do you think is going to happen in this industry? What actions do you think the industry leaders should take?
11. How do you evaluate business?
12. How do you judge a company when you are looking for a job?
13. Do you think your former employer is a well-managed organization?
14. Do you think a training program is useful? How do you evaluate a training program?
15. What have your read about our company or its products lately—outside of information in regular recruiting material?
16. You seem to have the analytical (financial, technical, etc.) skills. What makes you think you could handle the selling (line management, leadership, etc.) requirements of the job?
17. In addition to the company literature we sent out, to what sources did you go to find out about our corporation?
18. In your research on our company: (a) Do you see any specific problems we have? (b) Is there any division in our organization that you are most interested in?
19. Give me a good example of a good ad campaign (control program, mergers and acquisitions plan, etc.). Tell me why it's good.

20. Do you think it was a good move for us to divest our-selves of the _____ division?

21. What are the differences between an account manager's job and a product manager's job? A commercial lender and an investment banker? A financial analyst and a securities analyst? A consulting career versus a career with a corporation or a bank? Public accounting versus control?

22. I see that most of your experience has been in consumer products. How would you market a big-ticket item worth fifty thousand dollars?

23. Some interviewers may set up or describe a business situation and ask you to comment on it. Generally they're not looking for a pat answer but rather searching for common sense, logic, etc. Students who in prior years have reported that they did badly with this kind of question did so because they tried to give a "correct" answer rather than indicate what more they would like to know before giving an answer.

24. Based on this interview, what questions do you have about the company? What other questions might you have?

25. What can I tell you about our organization?

26. What do you think is a fair salary?

27. In your last job, what kinds of people (problems) annoyed you most? How did you deal with them?

LOCATION

1. Why do you want to stay in New York, locate to Chicago, etc.?

2. Are you free to relocate? What constraints do you have about relocation?

3. How do you feel about traveling? How does your family feel about traveling?
4. Do you mind the prospect of working abroad?

General Comments

Know Thyself!

1. Be prepared for open-ended interviews—where the interviewer does not ask many questions. Generally, this type of interviewer expects you to give an articulate and aggressive presentation, that is, how your knowledge and experience relate to the job in question and how you can contribute to the work of the firm. (They are really interested in finding out what you know about their business and why you want the particular job for which you are applying and whether you can perform it.)
2. Frequently, at the last interview of the day of the company visit, you may be questioned about how your day went, whom you saw, what you discussed, what impressed you, etc. You should have some notes as to what went on (names of people, their positions, topics covered) so you can discuss this intelligently.
3. Again and again, both in the initial and the follow-up interviews, you must be able to answer effectively: Why this industry? Why this job? Why our firm?
4. Women may be questioned more extensively about their motivation and direction, their aggressiveness, and their ability to handle a tough business situation.
5. Foreign nationals are often asked: How long can we expect you as an alien to work in the United States?

6. In general be prepared to explain, justify, and expand on everything you have in your résumé. Be able to identify a common thread throughout.

7. Remember, after each answer you give, the interviewer may very well ask, "Why?" Be prepared for this.

Have You Done Your Written Self-Analysis?

N.B. Aggressiveness as referred to on these pages does not mean abrasiveness. It means the ability to take charge and efficiently get the job done.

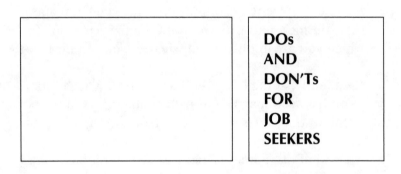

**DOs
AND
DON'Ts
FOR
JOB
SEEKERS**

Do

Stress your qualifications for the job opening.

Recount experience you have had which would fit you for the job.

Talk and think, so far as possible, about the future rather than the past.

Indicate, where possible, your stability, attendance record, and good safety experience.

Learn ahead of time about the company and its products. Do your homework.

Assume an air of confidence.

Approach the employer with respectful dignity.

Try to be optimistic in your attitude.

Maintain your poise and self-control.

Try to overcome nervousness or shortness of breath. (It helps to take a deep breath.)

Hold yourself erect.

Answer questions honestly and with straightforwardness.

Stress the contribution you can make to the enterprise.

Have a good résumé.

Apply for the job in person.

Let as many people as possible know you are job hunting.

Know the importance of getting along with people.

Recognize your limitations.

Make plenty of applications.

Indicate your flexibility and readiness to learn.

Be well groomed and appropriately dressed.

Don't

Keep stressing your need for a job.

Discuss past experience which has no application to the job situation.

Apologize for your age.

Be untidy in appearance.

Act overconfident.

Cringe or beg for consideration.

Speak indistinctly or with a muffled voice.

Be one of those who can do everything.

Hedge when answering questions.

Express your ideas on compensation, hours, etc., early in the interview.

Hesitate to fill out an application, give references, take a physical examination or tests on request.

Hang around, prolonging the interview, when it should be over.

Go to an interview without a record of your former work connections.

Arrive late and breathless for an interview.

Be a know it all or person who can't take instructions.

Isolate yourself from contacts who might help you find a job.

Feel that the world owes you a living.

Make claims about yourself that you cannot deliver on the job.

Display a feeling of inferiority.

CALLBACKS

A callback starts a whole new ball game as far as interviewing is concerned.

The first interview is relatively superficial. Recruiters are confirming what they read in your résumé, checking on your appearance and all of those things they can't discover via a résumé, appraising your interpersonal skills, and measuring how interested you really are in a job with their company. At the same time, they try to put together an attractive group of candidates that will conform to what hiring executives back at headquarters expect to see.

As a result, the first questions you are asked are relatively shallow, conversational, and unchallenging. Your job is to be polite, interested, well informed, and as personable as possible.

The callback usually consists of several interviewers— a senior executive in the personnel department who is often the first recruiter's boss; the manager of the department or departments where the new hirees will begin; an operating division head or other senior executive; and, sometimes, the chairman or president gets in on the fun.

By now, you have been rather fully screened. By attending the first interview, expressing real interest, and then accepting the callback, you have told the company that you seriously would like to get an offer from them. You are in the finals, or at least in the semifinals.

The general subject matter of the first interview now shifts to more specific issues. The nub of the questions moves from "Who are you?" and "What do you think?" to the more direct "What can you do?" and "How competitively competent do you think you'll be?" The personality contest is over and the digging for measurable values has begun.

Your job is to continue to be polite, interested, and charming; but here is where being well informed counts the most and here is where the quality and tenor of your questions become vital factors in getting a job offer.

I can't emphasize enough how important it is to have studied up on the company in such depth that you know everything that has been written in the past few annual reports, financial analyst reviews, and business publications. You know the company's organizational structure, its product and market break-outs, and its apparent opportunities and problems. You also know something about what its competitors are doing and where the industry is moving.

If you don't know these things and some of your fellow MBA interviewees do, then be prepared for a bullet. Go back and try again with another company and do it better.

If you have learned a lot about your candidate company, ask specific questions about their corporate strategy that are pertinent to the executive talking to you. Be careful not to be critical or flippant. Instead try to be so aware and so interested that the executive reacts by trying to give you reasons why you should join the company.

Similarly, when and if you have learned the corporate nuances of the interviewing company, you can do a much more effective job of asking about career paths, performance review policies, management development programs, and all of those things that are near and dear to the heart of a hopeful fast tracker.

A word of caution. Many of the executives you will talk to on callbacks were not fast trackers themselves. They became highly placed executives after a long tour of duty in jobs such as salesman, supervisor, foreman, and auditor. They may not be MBAs. They have a track record of specific achievements. They are proud of their values and you should respect them. Talk to the people in the personnel department all you want about fast tracks and fast trips, but be very careful in discussing this with successful operating executives.

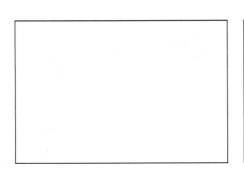

**DODGING
BULLETS**

When an MBA has an interview with a prospective employer—either at the school or after a callback to the company for a second round—and then receives a "Dear John" letter of rejection, in business school parlance, he was "shot down by a bullet."

The receipt of a bullet can be distressing and demoralizing to a person who has always been a scholastic star, a leader, a winner. "How could Goldman, Sachs (or General Mills or Exxon) turn me down? What am I doing wrong?" The receipt of several bullets in a row can compound the depression. The receipt of all bullets and no job offers—while one's fellow students are crowing over callbacks and offers—makes even the sturdiest MBA think of self-defenestration.

Before you jump out the window, review the bidding. At a single school, a company may interview forty students, call back only four, and hire two. That's a 10 percent and 5 percent yield. So if you had twenty interviews and received two callbacks and one job offer, you averaged out.

In most cases, the company sees many more MBAs than they can possibly call back and hire. They have a difficult time deciding which MBAs to include in the selected group since the line of demarcation is so narrow.

Don't lose your cool if at first you aren't called back. Keep plugging and stay confident. Wait for the percentages to catch up with you. I have seen many MBAs who have come up with superb job offers after receiving a spray of bullets from other companies.

However, if the bullets persist, it is well to pause and appraise your position. In retrospect, did you sense any pattern of resistance to your approach? You might want to talk things over with a counselor or someone in the placement division. Ask these questions:

Am I handling myself improperly or ineffectively? Did I mishandle any particular questions or issues? Was there something that made me uncomfortable? Was I too strong or too subdued?

If you are content that you are handling yourself appropriately, then keep hammering away for a few more interviews.

If you can figure out for yourself what's going wrong, then try to adjust your approach.

It is usually unwise to go back to interviewers who rejected you and ask them to give you the reasons; most of them are reluctant to be specific or to take the time unless there were unusual circumstances.

However, it is perfectly proper to ask the placement division to check with some interviewers whom they know well and who might give you a clue that will help you revise your approach.

The best armor against bullets, of course, is to go into your interviews completely prepared from every standpoint. Let a few bullets fly. They won't hurt you because you are going to win.

**WHAT
TO DO
WHEN
THE OFFER
COMES IN**

You have brought your interviews to a successful conclusion. Now it is the time to discuss the offer. Following are some suggestions from the Columbia Business School Placement Office, which should help this phase of your job search run as smoothly as possible.

Once an offer has been made (either verbally or in writing), make sure you understand all the specific details, i.e., salary, starting date, initial responsibilities, location, and *the date by which you must respond.* These details should be clearly understood, or they may cause problems later. Most organizations will give you a written confirmation of the offer. If this is not the potential employer's policy, it's all the more important that you clearly understand the details. (You may request something in writing if you feel uncomfortable with just a verbal agreement.)

THE RESPONSE DATE

Try to make sure that your response date gives you sufficient time to complete pending negotiations with other prospective employers. You want to make your decision with all the necessary facts on the table. However, this is the ideal situation. You may have to make an earlier decision than you would like. Let's be realistic. In all likelihood the sequence of initial interviews, callbacks, and offers will not follow the neat pattern you may desire. You may be at a callback stage with one organization you really like when an offer comes to you from another firm. This offer may come with a set response time not allowing you a chance to hear from other potential employers.

Your approach should be to notify the people who have extended you the offer and explain that you are very interested in the offer, but you have some discussions to complete. Ask for an extension of time and promise to get back to them by a specific date. Immediately call the other organizations with whom you are still dealing and explain the situation to them. Advise them that you would like to hear from them in time to make your decision. Be sure to impress upon them your interest in the position they are offering you and your desire to include them in your deliberations. The date you set with the first company should be considered a firm date, one that would be extremely difficult to renegotiate. So try to give yourself enough leeway when giving the other companies a date by which to tell you of their decision. Keep in mind, however, that because of the first organization's hiring schedule you may not receive an extension. In this case you must notify your other potential employers of this fact and ask for a decision as quickly as possible. Be prepared to have to make a decision before all the cards are dealt. Such a decision will be weighted by the perceived opportunity and your own gambling instincts.

THE STARTING DATE

If the company has a formal training program, the starting date will depend upon when that program begins. This may preclude your having a choice of starting dates. If you have a definite preference as to when you want to start, it is wise to speak up early. It should be clarified before you accept the offer. If you are an August graduate, be sure the company understands that you will not be available until after the summer term.

THE SALARY QUESTION

A company will often ask you what your salary expectations are—occasionally as early as the first interview. Thus it pays to give this some thought. A good research tool is the Salary Survey, which is prepared on the previous year's graduates. Salaries generally increase 7 percent to 10 percent a year. (After six months, 5 percent to 7 percent; and after a full year 7 percent to 10 percent.) Qualifications such as previous relevant work experience and a technical undergraduate degree, especially for jobs in the technological industries, will usually put you above the average. However, at best, it is difficult to guess what the company may be paying. You certainly don't want to sell yourself short. Nor do you want to miss an excellent career opportunity because your asking price is too high. Thus, in the early stages it is certainly wise to respond with a salary *range* indicating that pay is only one of the factors that you are considering, letting the employer know that the job and the opportunity are the important things. Consider the lower end of this range very carefully. It is difficult to negotiate upward later if you yourself give them a low salary that you would accept. Be sure that it is a figure you can live with. On the other hand, be sure the range you are talking about is relevant. Keep in mind that different industries have different salary ranges.

You may find yourself in a situation where a salary does become the critical factor and is lower than you feel you can accept. Negotiations for a higher salary are possible. The Salary Survey, offering some other organizations' figures for a comparable position, may be used as ammunition in negotiations. However, there are other things you should consider: Why do you want to negotiate? Is this a job you really want, or are you just playing games? Is it peer pressure? Is it false pride? Are you worth more, really? You must think of this worth in terms of the organization, the job, and yourself when you negotiate. The real name of the game is to get the position you want with a fair and equitable salary. It is best to ease into salary negotiations. Explore the situation to see whether it is negotiable. "The job offer is giving me some trouble—could we discuss it?" When you get into these negotiations it is important to think in terms of the total job package, not just the salary. You may bring other things into it, such as work conditions, increased job responsibilities and/or exposure, and a shorter training program. Before you get into the negotiations, make sure you understand fully the firm's compensation package, raise policy, bonus, and fringe benefits. Also make sure you know what it is you feel you have to merit the higher price tag (i.e., what your strengths and abilities are that make you worth the higher salary). It is not wise to negotiate more than one offer at a time. Be careful not to back yourself into a corner should the company be unwilling to negotiate. Further pressure could only cause ill feelings and although the company will not likely retract its offer, it could make for an unpleasant beginning on your new job. Never try to force a higher offer by quoting a fabricated figure from another organization. Besides being dishonest, the resulting fallout could severely damage your professional reputation. The business community is much more closely knit than it seems.

SOME GENERAL RULES TO FOLLOW

1. Keep your lines of communication open with all potential employers.
2. Once you have ruled out an organization, let them know. The earlier this can be done in the job-hunting process, the better. It opens up jobs for your classmates.
3. Once you have accepted an offer, contact any company by whom you are still being considered and tell them of your decision. Open up the job lines for others.
4. When you accept the job, it is best to follow up any personal or phone contact with a confirmation letter.

Evaluat-
ing Jobs

CORPORATE CULTURE

Corporate culture may be characterized as "the way we do things abound here" (Marvin Bower, McKinsey & Company).

"Corporate culture" runs high on the list of significant MBA buzzwords these days. People use the phrase in various ways, but fundamentally it means what a company believes in and stands for, what kind of values it places on certain procedures and traditions and, to a certain extent, what kind of management style is formed by the reigning executive corps.

It is easy to perceive the contrast in corporate culture between the laid-back Apple Computer and the rather formal IBM, for example. These companies tend to attract different types of people who wish to work in sharply opposing climates. This is not to say that one is better than the other.

Corporate cultures vary, but not as sharply, between Procter & Gamble and General Foods, Westinghouse and General Electric, Bloomingdale's and Sears, General Motors and Volvo, Morgan Stanley and Salomon Brothers, and so on.

There is usually a gulf of cultural differences between the large, public, citified Mobil and the smaller Southwestern closely controlled oil company. There are geographical differences between companies such as Caterpillar, Dow, and Corning Glass, whose headquarters are in smaller cities, and some of their counterparts in large metropolitan centers, just as there are differences between Los Angeles, Raleigh–Durham, Boston, and Minneapolis. There is a totally different working atmosphere in a Silicon Valley start-up company than at Bethlehem Steel, or at Tiffany's as compared to your local used-car dealer.

Picking the right corporate culture for your career to thrive in cannot be done by formula. It is a matter of taste. You should observe it and try to sample it before you commit to a long-term decision. What if there is a mixture of cultures, such as may be found in certain conglomerates? Don't cultures sometimes change radically with management succession changes? Corporate culture is a dynamic matter. It does evolve and shift just as entire companies and industries alter their basic focus and structure over the years.

As an MBA, I don't think I would choose one company over another only because I liked its corporate culture better. To me, strategic thrust, track record, industry reputation, and management-development policies are more important. On the other hand, it *is* a matter to be considered, and, if I felt that I might be uncomfortable within a particular corporate culture, it would contribute to my deciding against it.

The important thing to remember is that the environment you move into is a stronger force than you are. It will not change to accommodate you. You cannot afford to clash so strongly with the environment that you appear to be out of step or opposed to it. If you want to be accepted and become part of the team, you probably have to learn how to conform to the prevailing corporate culture. If you don't want to conform to a given environment, then don't take the job.

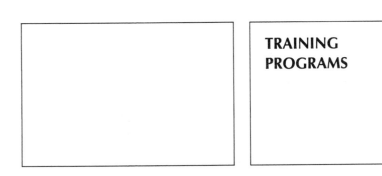

TRAINING PROGRAMS

In evaluating the merits of going with one company or another, an MBA has lots of things to think about, among the most important: company reputation, training record, and personnel policy. One that is often overlooked, ignored, or minimized is the presence of a high-quality training program.

I realize that many MBAs feel that the last thing in the world they want after their all-out B-school stint is to get more training. And lots of companies feel that after they have paid that high salary to an MBA, they want him or her to go to work pronto.

As a new managerial candidate employee you should be given a thorough briefing of the corporate picture—its history, principles, politics, procedures, and organization. The primary business or businesses should be comprehended from the standpoint of products, markets, and competitive thrust. Plants and marketing facilities should be visited. Key executives should be met. The new employee has to get to know the company before he or she can properly take pride in it.

You'll learn more in your first six months at your new company than in your next five years. Don't miss the chance of including a formal training program in that period.

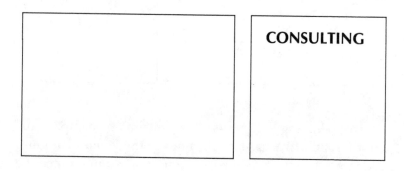

CONSULTING

Some of my best friends are management consultants, but that still doesn't keep me from believing that MBAs are usually better off by *not* accepting those gorgeous offers from McKinsey, Booz • Allen, and the Boston Consulting Group.

The lure of the job offer is almost irresistible. They seem to say, "Come to us and work closely with great companies and great executives on great problems of great scope. Let us teach you to become a skilled problem solver, interviewer, writer, and presenter. Gain breadth of experience. Travel. Stay with us and become a wealthy partner. Or consult yourself into a high-level job with a client."

When this is added to a fifty-thousand-dollar-plus pay-check, and only the smartest MBAs are invited, it's a hard offer to turn down, and most MBAs grab for it.

Management consultants want these smart MBAs and are willing to pay high salaries to get them because they can get their money's worth out of them almost from the start. The MBA selected is a superior writer, presenter, and problem solver with good interpersonal skills. The consulting firm can put him or her to work right away on project teams with experienced consultants and bill their clients at a rate that will bring a profit. The consulting firm expects that it will have high turnover, with two to five years being the typical job tenure.

In some ways, it appears to be a win/win situation. The consultant services his clients well and makes a profit. The MBA makes excellent money and gains wide experience.

Nevertheless, in many cases, I believe that MBAs fail to think through the reasons for taking a consulting job.

In the first place, the work isn't always going to be glamorous. Only occasionally does it bring the young MBA into the chairman's New York office to help reorganize divisions, create a new international strategy, or devise a whole new pricing theory. More often it means working with a troubled division or company that needs relatively routine new procedures or programs set up, and you get to live five weeks in a motel in the boondocks while you're developing the report. You usually can't control the types of products, markets, companies, or services you are as-signed to work on, so the experience gained may not be pertinent to what you ultimately want to do.

A bigger problem is the next job. If you want to make management consulting your lifetime career, fine and dandy. But most MBAs go into counseling as a step for their next job. Regrettably, my observation is that it usually turns out to be another "consulting type" job.

This is because the most logical next step for someone with two to five years of consulting firm experience is to go into strategic planning or to do in-house consultation for a corporation. This is usually highly paid work to be sure, but it is staff work where one either eventually plateaus out at a high level or, again, must "consult himself" into a more significant administrative post with the corporation. Since he has had little or no administrative or supervisory experience and since he has only made recommendations for others to execute, he has an extremely difficult time finding an appropriate and available slot to fit into.

Take his MBA classmate who started with the corporation in the first place. He now has from five to ten years of managerial track record, is a known quantity and probably has a brighter future with the corporation.

"But think of all the management consultants who blossomed into major corporate leaders," rebut my MBA friends. "Look at John Macomber of Celanese, Andrall Pearson of Pepsico, Charles Knight of Emerson Electric. Here are three examples of men with consulting backgrounds who made it to the top as chairman or president of a large corporation."

My guess is that if we take the top five earners in the thousand companies in the United States we will perhaps find as many as fifty people who began their career as management consultants. But we will find more than four thousand who began their careers in a marketing, operations, or control job with that company or a similar company. Why buck the odds?

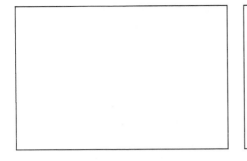

THE INTERNATIONAL JOB

One of the most popular career preferences expressed by entering MBAs is for international work. Although usually described in somewhat vague terms, the desire is to spend a few years working in a foreign country (a developed nation, please) and then to return to a managerial position in the U.S. headquarters office dealing with the foreign operations.

There is often some reason behind this desire—fluency in a foreign language or having lived extensively abroad, for example. More often, it is just an urge brought on by a liking for travel, or stimulus from a junior year spent in Italy.

However, there just aren't many attractive international jobs open to MBAs anymore. The overseas arena is not what it was ten years ago. Most American multinational companies now staff their foreign posts almost exclusively with foreign nationals, many of whom have been put through training courses at U.S. operating bases. These local people have often studied in the U.S. or England and may have an MBA in addition to fluency in English.

There are some notable exceptions. Large commercial banks continue to encourage a tour of duty in a foreign branch for their highly regarded executive comers. The oil companies, the wide-ranging construction firms, and high technology businesses still have many Americans in their outpost offices. But this amounts to a small number of job openings each year.

The way to get involved in an international career with an American-based multinational company these days is to become a successful manager in a domestic operating division and then arrange to be transferred to a managerial or coordinating assignment in the international headquarters. And learn a language well! You will probably be disappointed, however, if you count on finding an appropriate international job with a major company right after graduation. I am of course generalizing here. I have seen dozens of exceptions.

Susan, who was fluent in Mandarin Chinese and had taught for two years in Taiwan, had offers from four banks to join their Pacific divisions. Vicky, who also spoke Chinese, found a fine job in W. R. Grace's international purchasing department. John, who had worked two summers in Hong Kong, was hired by General Electric's International Trading Corporation. Carlos, with relatives in Brazil and a fluency in both Spanish and Portuguese, has started his own importing business in New York City. Notice they all spoke at least one other language. Bob, through sheer persistence, has organized an international-licensing service in New York City.

For each of these MBAs who found an international outlet for their desires and talents, I know of a dozen who have been frustrated and disappointed. They found no job in their field, or took a job where there was inadequate scope or stimulation and had to start over again a year or two later.

If you are just starting your MBA program and have

that international yearning, it may be appropriate to switch your concentration to marketing or finance, perhaps, and load up on internationally flavored electives.

I'm trying to be realistic, not discouraging. I believe that virtually all major corporations must become accomplished global operators; that there is almost no such thing anymore as a purely domestic decision; and that the future CEOs of our leading American companies have to acquire international breadth and know-how.

Many of our American executives will learn how to do business around the world by attending foreign meetings, by taking a few special courses and by sitting in on a variety of negotiations and dealings. How much better off they would be if they had a foreign tour of duty under their belts along with some language fluency.

Don't give up. Just recognize that it takes creative digging to find the kind of international job opening you want and that it might be a two-stage process.

TWO-STAGE JOBS

It's sometimes hard for students to realize that it takes two and three moves for them to get into the type of work they want to do. Take venture capital, for example, where hundreds of MBAs each year contemplate applying for jobs. (The lure here is that the general partners in successful venture capital firms have been able to make big money in recent years.)

There are perhaps two hundred venture capital partnerships in the U.S. today and they are inundated each year with thousands of MBA résumés, letters, and calls. My guess is that they hire fewer than a dozen of the applicants. They prefer people with venture capital or closely related experience who come in as general partners or senior associates or who organize wholly new firms. So how does one get this experience?

Well, there are perhaps another hundred venture capital operations in the U.S. that are affiliated with banks, investment banking firms, and corporations. These firms tend to pay attractive salaries and bonuses to effective workers, but not the likes of what the outstanding general partners can make. A typical career path, then, is to learn the venture capital trade and build a reputation with a commercial firm and then branch out entrepreneurially. A similar move may be made after gaining experience in certain areas of investment banking, corporate planning, and financial analysis.

It isn't all that easy for an MBA to get a job directly with the venture capital division of First Chicago or Smith Barney, for example. These are sought-after posts, and the young strivers who are in the commercial or corporate finance areas of such companies are hammering on the doors, saying, "When you have an opening, take me first."

Therefore, before you can make it big as a venture capitalist, you may have to pass through two or three experience-building stages—and that's probably as it should be. The point is to recognize this situation early and plan your life accordingly.

There are quite a few other attractive areas that have similar multistage career paths—strategic planning, fund management, product management, and international marketing, to name a few. MBAs can't usually go directly into these fields; they must become proficient in another one first.

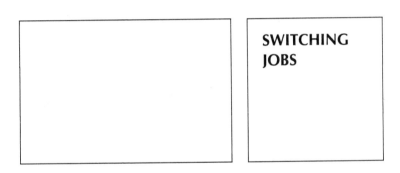

SWITCHING JOBS

Lots of people voluntarily switch jobs during their business careers. (I've worked for six companies.) The reason they do so, almost invariably, is to improve their situation and to enhance their opportunities. But it doesn't always work out that way.

The main reason for so many job-switching tap-outs is that people don't look broadly enough at the full package being offered them. I think there are six elements that must be present or the job switch is in jeopardy:

1. Broader responsibility over more functions or activities or volume.

2. Higher title.
3. Higher level on organization chart (nearer to the CEO).
4. High salary.
5. Better short- and long-term bonuses and option opportunities.
6. Better long-term promotion opportunities (and this takes some probing and a certain amount of guessing to ascertain).

Whenever a person moves to a new company, there is a significant element of risk involved. You should have an effective risk/reward ratio going for you.

If you are missing one or more of these six elements, be extremely wary.

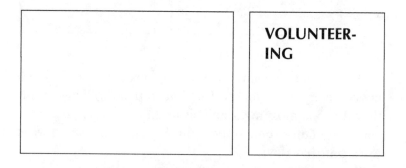

VOLUNTEER-ING

In the navy, the old veterans counseled us new recruits, "Never volunteer for anything." That may have been good advice for the armed services, and perhaps for the civil service, but exactly the opposite philosophy goes in the business world.

What kinds of things do you volunteer for? Damned near everything.

When a task force or project team is being formed to work on a tough problem or a new idea or a change of some type, try to get assigned to it. (Clear it with your boss, of course!) If the group has already been announced, try to get added—even if you don't make it they'll remember you the next time around. You'll have an interesting, high-profile experience working with other high-performance people.

When there's a real mess at hand, volunteer to work on it. You might be able to help clean it up and, if so, reap credit. You may end up burying a dead horse, but if you conduct an efficient, expeditious funeral service, you will be recognized as someone who does hard jobs right.

Volunteer to head up the United Way drive, to work the booth at the convention, to come in after the flood, to escort foreign visitors, to write the minutes of the meeting, to teach in the training school. It shows that you are vigorous, interested and, probably, an overachiever.

A word or two of caution, however. Do your own job first and do it very well. If you are behind in your quota or your in-box, don't run the Christmas party. And don't do too much fringe-type volunteer work. Concentrate your volunteering on tasks which are immediately related to product, market, and management experience gains.

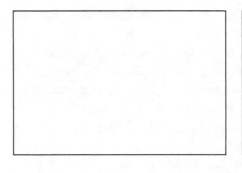

THE ROTATIONAL EXPERIENCE

Companies are greatly concerned these days about having their senior executives equipped with the broadest possible range of skills. The reason is simple. At the top of a large corporation one must deal competently with *all* of the business trades—finance, marketing, operations, control, planning, research, public relations—everything. Executives who have become too specialized in one segment either do not get chosen for a top slot or have an extremely difficult indoctrination and adjustment period.

Most thoughtful companies treat this as a continuing matter of interest and concern. They constantly send their upwardly mobile managers to training schools and to executive education programs, frequently in anticipation of a promotion to a new and broader assignment. To a certain extent, also, the organization chart fulfills this function as orderly progression to each new level brings a new scope of responsibilities.

Standard operating practice, however, usually goes far beyond this and involves a conscious program of job rotation. This may involve a tour of duty in the headquarters office for the field operating division comers. They learn the corporate viewpoint, get to know the corporate staffers with whom they will be dealing, and get looked over by the top executives.

A typical rotational headquarters assignment for a field operating executive is in the corporate planning department working on the strategic future of the corporation. Or it could involve work in financial analysis, or on capital projects, or on special projects or task forces.

It is a two-way street, as well, since some selected corporate staffers need to be given operating business experience. This is harder to do, since there are not many operating jobs that can be stepped into without specific background—and it's another reason why corporate career paths that start in the operating divisions are easier to follow than those which start at headquarters.

Most of our multinational corporations want their top executives to have worked directly with foreign problems at some time during their career. This is particularly true of the big banks, the companies with worldwide manufacturing and marketing integration, and those with significant export business. If you go to work for a company where this is a standard pattern, start clamoring early for a foreign assignment or for international experience. There are more good learning jobs available at the lower levels and you are not yet encumbered with the problems of children, schools, mortgage, and other similar issues.

The most frequent pattern of rotational learning takes place in the mainstream of business where a conscious, concerted effort is made to develop better, broader managers. There are many ways to do it. I especially like the ways three companies go about it—all quite different.

- General Electric is fundamentally organized around some 350 profit centers, called Strategic Business Units (SBU).

An early goal at General Electric is to get fast trackers trained to manage an SBU, where they are exposed to marketing, manufacturing, and control supervisory responsibility and can be measured quantitatively as to results. Basically, the GE theory is that after successfully managing a small SBU, one can be moved to manage another, larger SBU in a different product or market area and then to managing groups of SBUs.

- IBM runs its company (and beautifully) on a more function-oriented basis, but with regular, almost continuous, reorganizations as products, markets, and conditions change. Without the GE SBUs, IBM moves its top young sales employees and operating people into jobs such as a product manager position, where they acquire broader knowledge and work closely with other people on project teams and task forces. Although the successful IBMers can usually be judged quantitatively on performance, they may never have had clear-cut profit responsibility until reaching the CEO slot.

- 3M prides itself on the early recognition and development of executives through work on new products. At 3M, new ventures are constantly being organized to appraise, exploit, and launch a new product which ultimately may blossom into a full operating division. As young people gain experience in their operating jobs at 3M, they become increasingly eligible to join and to participate in these new venture groups.

Every good company has its own way of identifying its high-potential people and getting them on the fast track as soon as possible. Because of their well-rounded education and maturity, MBAs are unusually well qualified to compete under such circumstances where knowledge of the complete business operation is important.

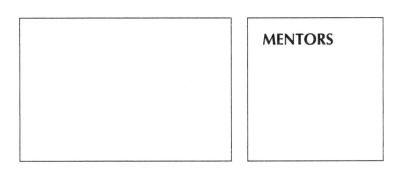

MENTORS

A mentor is an executive who takes a young person under his or her wing at a company and offers guidance, counseling, and support.

At some companies this is an organized system. More frequently, it is an informal method of sponsorship.

Sometimes, it is the executive who takes the initiative and builds an entourage of upwardly mobile young people. One example is a rotating post for administrative assistant. Other times, the young person manages to meet an executive and induces him or her to function as an informal mentor.

There may be times, I suppose, when a mentor can be very helpful and useful, particularly in a company where there is a planned effort. Generally speaking, however, I don't like the idea.

To begin with, the young newcomer tends to hitch his

or her wagon to the mentor's star. If the mentor falters or leaves or is resented by his peers, the new person suffers through shared identification. If the mentor rises and carries the young friend(s) along, many observers jealously contend that favor-currying did it for them and not talent and effective work.

Don't turn a kindly mentor off; he or she invariably means well and can be helpful if used sparingly. Do keep your head and build your own reputation on deeds.

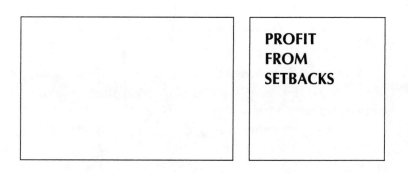

PROFIT FROM SETBACKS

Most MBAs have never really met with failure. They were highly successful in high school and college. Usually, they were class officers, club leaders, fine athletes, and scholarship winners. They held a few pleasant summer jobs. Their work after college often began with a training program and then moved into closely supervised work with little delegated authority.

At business school, they continued to get good grades, to be leaders in school activities, to hold down educational summer jobs—and they were hired by a fine company.

In the real world, where you have authority and responsibility, there will be many times when you fail, regardless of how hard and smart you work. It can be because of a product failure, a competitor's move, a bad strategy forced upon you, an error made by someone you counted on.

Business executives know that every active doer fails frequently (Babe Ruth struck out 1,330 times, you know). What they are interested in is how you react to failure. Do you whimper, mope, and finger-point? Or do you get up off the floor and go on the attack again with vigor, learning from your experience?

That's why good companies try to put their fast trackers as quickly as possible in a job or on an assignment where they can be fire tested. They want to find out how you are going to perform in a crisis when the chips are down and when errors and failures can be rather quickly overcome. They don't want to go through a long waiting period while you are doing staff work and making recommendations to other people—and then find out you don't perform well in a crisis situation.

When opportunity knocks, answer the door. You may be in for one of the most important learning experiences you'll ever have.

How Jim Got His Job

This is a true story. Jim came to Columbia Business School because he had worked in a commercial bank in Boston for three years and had seen MBAs come into his bank and get right on the fast track. He didn't think they were any smarter than he was, but they spoke a different language, seemed to know a few new tricks, and exuded a confidence he didn't have.

So he marched off to business school with the idea that he would return to commercial banking with new credentials and a new start on the same fast track.

During his first year, he began to put together a list of the banks in the country he thought he might want to work for. He read their annual reports and the major banking magazines. He went to all the lectures and affairs at the school where banking was the primary subject. And he got a summer job at a big New York City bank.

During his third term, he arranged to visit Columbia graduates in the eight biggest banks in New York City and talked with them about the bank's personnel policies, working climate, directional thrust, and competitive posture. During his midterm breaks, he did the same thing in Boston and Pittsburgh. At Christmas, he visited banks in Chicago, Los Angeles, and San Francisco.

After each interview (having had more than one at several banks), he typed out his notes and stapled the card of the person interviewed to the pages. He put his fifteen "call reports" into a notebook along with short financial summaries of the banks.

He took this notebook with him as he finally interviewed all fifteen of the banks, ten through the school and five by direct personal application. None of the interviewers had ever before seen an MBA candidate so knowledgeable about the banking industry, or so prepared to talk about their individual bank.

Jim received excellent job offers from *all fifteen* of the banks, with several of his interviewers pursuing him with persistence.

Charlie's Job Search

After graduating from a leading Ivy League university, Charlie was hired by a distinguished Wall Street banking house. After two years, he received a hefty salary increase and was promoted to a managerial position which gave him a lot of authority along with room to grow.

Charlie, however, was concerned that he did not have the educational credentials for his long-term aspiration of becoming a senior partner at his firm. He considered going to night school for his MBA, but felt that it would conflict with his heavy work program, would take too long, and would unsettle his family life. (His wife had a career and they already had little enough time together.)

He told his company that he was contemplating enrolling at Columbia Business School. After discussing the pros and cons, they wished him well and urged him to keep in close touch while at school.

At school, Charlie got good grades and got a great deal out of the experience. He also took on some projects at his company during his midterm and semester breaks. And he regularly checked in with his former supervisors and associates.

When it came time to sign up for interviews, Charlie went to his firm and said, "My MBA experience has reconvinced me that I was in the right profession and that I have been working for the right company. May we talk now about my returning?"

They promptly made him an offer that was as good as or better than what he could have gotten from anyone else. Charlie equally promptly accepted it. He then canceled all of his interviews and spent his final school term concentrating on his class work.

Is he confident that he did the right thing? Is he happy now?

Charlie says, "I am now in position to work with confidence and competitively without any limitations in the company. I learned what I needed to learn. And it was a positive cash investment."

Was Charlie right to handle his job search in this fashion? Should he have interviewed some other companies to explore alternatives?

In Charlie's exact circumstances, I think he did the right thing. He was in the industry he wanted to be in and with a company he liked, and where he was liked. To have looked at competitive businesses would have proved little. So I agreed with him—and I also was pleased that he did not want to take interviews away from his classmates or time away from his own classes.

On the other hand, had Charlie been less certain of his situation at his former employer and less secure in his belief that he was working for an outstanding company, then I would have urged him to get a "second opinion." This would have let him firm up his feelings or, at least, have a look at another option with little time cost.

Susan's Second Job Hunt

Susan was fascinated with computers, especially the software side. She majored in finance at business school, but also took all the computer-related electives she could find. She did well at school, getting Dean's List grades and being elected an officer of the student association. She had several job offers and took one as a financial analyst with a high-technology firm in the West.

Her job was to analyze the potential success for new product and market developments of her company, to review problem situations and recommend solutions, and to assist in looking into new ventures for her company to invest in. It was interesting work and closely related to her skills.

As the months wore on in her job, Susan felt that she was not heading toward any challenging goal. She was making lots of recommendations to other people that were well received, but she was not making any decisions herself, nor was she managing anything or anybody, and she could not see clearly what her next job would be in the company.

Meanwhile, she had seen some venture capitalists at work. They seemed to be having fun and making money and did not have as good a background as she. So she resigned from her company and went back to New York City to look for a venture capital job.

She was professional in her job-hunting approach. She updated her résumé, putting emphasis on the school and work experiences that were relevant to the venture capital business.

She scoured the financial magazines and developed an up-to-date list of all of the venture capital firms, divisions, and partnerships in the greater New York City area. She set up a card file on each firm showing capitalization, partner information, and references to any deals the firm had been involved in.

Early on, she came to Columbia Business School and checked in with the alumni placement office and her faculty friends. Through these contacts she was able to get introductions to a few of the leading venture capitalists.

Most of her interviews—and she had dozens of them —came through her own hard work. Writing letters, making phone calls, following leads, talking with financially oriented acquaintances, classmates, and alumni.

Although she was attractive, smart, polite, energetic, well educated, and had related experience, she had a very hard time getting a venture capital job and it took a long time and it cost her a lot of money.

What did Susan do wrong? Several things.

First, she leaped before she looked. She decided that she wanted to be a venture capitalist before she found out about the career paths. People get to be venture capitalists by making several logical moves through commercial- or investment-banking channels. They build a reputation and a following so that they are attractive as a general partner or a firm founder. There are very few openings available for twenty-seven-year-old MBAs with two years of work experience as a high-tech company financial analyst.

Second, she didn't realize that she was much more interesting as a job candidate while she was employed than while she was unemployed. People and companies prefer to hire people away from someone else and are suspicious of a resigner.

Third, she didn't calculate the dangers of not finding a venture capital job right away. Not only did she lose time and money, but she lost her shelf freshness. After two or three months of job hunting, it is hard to explain why you are still looking and it's even harder to keep a positive, upbeat attitude.

Finally, she overestimated her ability to sell herself. She had always been good at sales and successful in her beginning jobs, in school politics, in her extracurricular activities. But when she tried to crack a tough, tight, money-hungry, limited-access industry, she didn't have enough power or the right game plan.

The sequel to the story is that she found a beginning venture capitalist who took her on as an unpaid fund raiser. She found that she was good at this because she had learned so much about the venture capital business during her job search. So she quickly sold herself, this time on a salaried basis, to a larger firm where she began to work on ventures as well as fund raising. She is now officially launched on her desired career.

Peter's Problem

After three years of sales work for a packaged-foods company, Peter went for his MBA to better prepare himself for a managerial career in marketing. He did well at school, getting good grades and enjoying a number of interesting side activities.

As a summer job, he worked on a project team of five

students who did field research work for a professor who was writing a book on strategic planning. When the work was not finished at summer's end, Peter took an additional term off and finished up the project. By this time he had concluded that he would like to go for a marketing management career with a company manufacturing an industrial product as opposed to a consumer packaged item—and I encouraged him to do so.

He was hired by a prominent paper company and put through a short but intensive training program with several other trainees, mostly with bachelor's degrees. He was assigned to a midwestern district sales office with the parting words, "We are watching your progress. As soon as it is appropriate, we'll pull you back for a tour of duty in the strategic planning department or begin training you to be a product manager."

About two years later, his company merged with another major paper producer and their two sales organizations were consolidated. Peter was transferred to a larger regional office and given somewhat broader sales responsibility. Unfortunately the two executives at headquarters who knew him best were shifted to other positions. Even more unfortunately, in a cost-cutting move, a cutback was made in the headquarters staff and the number of job openings became fewer.

After four years in field sales, Peter has been told to hang in there and keep trying to improve his performance, but no clear timetable has been set for his promotion to headquarters.

Did Peter make a mistake? I don't think so. He was caught in the middle of a merger and a reorganization, but that seems to happen to a number of people these days.

He still works for a leading company in an enormous industry where great long-term executive opportunities exist. He has learned much about his product, market, and practices. He is well thought of by his supervisors and is considered a valuable asset.

If his present employer does not give him the job satisfaction he needs and deserves, then he should have no qualms about moving to another company which will give him the advancement he deserves. He may have been delayed, but it is a momentary slowdown and he will find success.

Bill's Game Plan

Shortly after I met him, Bill told me that he wanted to run an industrial corporation some day. He took all the courses at business school he felt could help most in an operating management career. He had good leadership qualities and was the president of two school organizations.

Because he was personable, smart, and competitive, Bill was offered callbacks and jobs by almost every company he interviewed. I told him that he should feel flattered, but his contention was that he was simply justifying the faith that his parents had when they invested in his business school tuition and he needed to think clearly as to which offer to select.

After thorough discussion, he turned down the ones which had staff-work overtones and gave primary consideration to those which gave him specific product and functional training. His final selection was to begin a year's session as administrative assistant to the president of an operating division of a chemical company. As I said earlier, I tell MBAs to be wary of "assistant to" jobs as a rule.

However, Bill found that earlier holders of these positions at his chosen company had moved quickly and directly to supervisory jobs, so he went ahead. And now he is positive that he made the right job decision.

Stella's Switch

Stella was one of our most popular students. She liked to be with people and talk to them about their aspirations.

Before coming to the MBA program, she had been involved in personnel work with a bank in New York City. She began to feel dead-ended and feared being typed as a personnel specialist.

At the school she took a double concentration in management of organizations and in finance. Her primary idea was to follow the crowd and go into investment banking. As she began to get passing grades in her finance courses and top grades in the management of organization courses, she started to question her career objective.

"I want to be where the action is," she told me, "but I'm getting queasy about my ability to compete in the corporate finance or the sales and trading department of an investment banking firm. What am I to do?"

After talking a while, she concluded that she should lead from her strength and go for a job in the human resources department of an investment banker. With the broader base from her MBA, she would not be limited to the degree that she found in her earlier work experience.

She found almost exactly what she was looking for with a commercial bank (not her former employer) who was making a strong move into the capital markets field and needed a human resources coordinator.

She likes her job a lot. She works closely with the key

executives and deal-makers, but concentrates on organizational planning, compensation packaging, and recruiting. She is not dragging down a million-dollar salary but she makes more than twice her pre-MBA salary, is in the midst of the excitement, and is getting great job satisfaction.

Larry the Loser

After twenty-six interviews at and through the school, Larry had not received a single job offer and had only one callback interview at the recruiter's office. It was two months after graduation when Larry came to see me for the first time. My questions went something like this:

Q. What was your concentration?
A. I ended up with finance, but I switched from marketing in my third term.
Q. Whom did you interview?
A. I started off with trying for investment banking jobs, but when I bombed out in my interviews, I began signing up to see marketing recruiters.
Q. How were your grades?
A. Not very good. Nothing above a pass. But I had no failures.
Q. What activities were you in at school?
A. I played on the rugby team for awhile.
Q. Did you take the communications course and have practice sessions on videotape?
A. I didn't know they were available.
Q. What would you say your objective is right now?
A. To get a job. Any kind of a job.

This sounds exaggerated, but it is a true story. Larry,

and an unfortunate few like him, used their MBA-getting time as an opportunity to avoid work for a couple of years.

Happily, Larry pulled his socks up, swallowed his pride, and got himself into a sales training program at a fairly good company, but at about the same salary level he held before school. He is sadder, and it remains to be seen if he is wiser.

Pat's Course

As a music major at an Eastern liberal arts college, Pat had little or no concept of a business career when he graduated. So he spent three delightful years researching the history of music in a midwestern city through a government grant. During this time, he began to realize that he would, some day, inherit a sizable sum of money from his parents, and he had no idea how to handle it.

After discussing several alternatives, he decided to apply for his MBA. Somewhat to his surprise, as well as his parents', he turned out to be an excellent student and became very interested in the process of business.

His career goal became that of owning and managing a company small enough so that he could participate in all phases of it, but large enough to need some of the things he was learning at business school.

When McKinsey offered him a consulting job, it seemed to fit well with his objectives. He would gain practical experience and be exposed to a variety of companies; he had a chance to grow and mature and prepare himself for a later opportunity that he could create.

At the end of his first year, when I checked with him, he felt that he had made the right job decision. He liked his work and he was beginning to formulate his plans for an entrepreneurial move. I'm confident that he will do it right.

Jack's Extra Effort

Not only was Jack one of the best school "politicians" I have ever seen, he was also a good student and a person who got things done.

By virtue of spirited campaigning, he got himself elected as president of the student government association in the fall term of his second year. During that time he organized a symposium to discuss student government and invited students from twenty other business schools to attend, which they all did.

He talked one of the leading packaged-foods corporations in the country into sponsoring the symposium and underwriting a significant share of the travel costs involved. It was a highly successful operation and is now a continuing annual event. Jack turned in a fine performance as conference leader and made many friends.

When he graduated with honors and a marketing concentration, Jack went to work for—you guessed it—his symposium sponsor.

Adam's Approach

Two years after getting his MBA, Adam was out of a job. Actually he was out of two jobs, because his first assignment after getting his MBA was with a financial service group that failed and his next post was with a firm that did not give him the work he was hired to do. When I saw him, he was distraught.

After reviewing his experiences, my conclusion was that

he had not properly thought through his job objectives nor had he been thorough in his original job search. He had simply taken two job offers that sounded good and paid well, but had too little substance.

I urged him to start all over with his self-appraisal, his work interests, and a new list of employer prospects. He did a fine job of reorganization and within two months he was back at work with a substantial financial services company and embarked upon a new career that he felt had solid long-term prospects. I asked him to write out for me what he learned from this experience; here's a digest of what he said:

USE THE FOUR Ps

PERSONALITY   Develop a list of the key people in the industry and the companies where you want to work. Sell yourself to them. Keep in contact.

PRESENTATION   Stress your positive accomplishments and all you have learned in your previous jobs.

PREPARATION   Do your homework before every call. Do it intensively.

PERSISTENCE   Keep after the industry, the firm, the people you want to work with. You're not just looking for a job; you are building a career.

Nice going, Adam.

Looking Back: A Summary

When my business friends ask me, "What do you say to those MBAs to whom you talk at Columbia School? What advice do you give them?" the answer is, of course, all of the things that I have written in this book, as well as a great deal of highly individualized counseling in special situations. There isn't any short and simple answer that applies across the board.

In looking back over all of my notes, however, I think I have been consistent in suggesting these first six steps:

1. Do a thorough job of self-analysis regarding your strengths and weaknesses as well as your likes and dislikes, and then try to match yourself up with the type of industry, company, and job that seems best fit for you.

2. Take full advantage of all the offerings of your business school. Learn from the placement division, the library, the alumni network, your interested faculty members, the visiting business people. Never stop asking questions about careers, career goals, and career paths.

3. As you begin to home in on what appears to be the most logical area for a career concentration, exercise some initiative and creativity. Don't confine yourself to talking with companies who come to the school. The

best jobs may well be with those thousands of companies who do not interview at your school. Seek them out and check them out.

4. Prepare diligently for each of your interviews. Review your approach and your presence. Hone your interpersonal skills. Do special research when possible. Keep positive and upbeat.

5. When finally selecting an entry job, take time to think of all aspects. Appraise the previous experience of MBAs in the same arena. Consider the long-term aspects, especially the second or third career post. Compare the company's culture with your own values.

6. Always keep building on your MBA base. Never stop studying and learning. Stay in touch with your school. Become part of the alumni network. Stay current and curious and keep growing.

The above six points are general and simplified. Your own case is much more detailed and complicated and deserves special care and attention.

The career determination process is a dynamic one. From the time you begin thinking about your career until you make a final choice, many things will happen. The world will change, companies will change, *you* will change. The time during which you are at business school gives you a marvelous opportunity to think deeply about what you want to do with the rest of your life.

It isn't easy to do this by yourself, so don't be afraid to seek the advice and counsel of older, experienced business executives who will help you make the best decisions a little sooner and a little more surely than you might alone.

Who knows, the counseling you receive may be a key factor in converting your MBA into a CEO!

Appendix

Making
the Most
of Alumni
Counseling
Board
Interviews

Your meeting with members of the Alumni Counseling Board will help you learn about the various industries, functional areas, and individual jobs in which you are interested, and thus to clarify and strengthen your career plans before your permanent job interviews begin. These meetings are deliberately informal in nature, as described in the following passage from a letter from the Columbia Business School Placement Office inviting alumni to join the board:

> The format is simple and low-key. A student asks for an appointment at a time and place convenient to you. The discussion is to be purely informative and exploratory and thus the pressures and constraints of employment interviews are avoided. Students are as interested in the frustrations as they are in the satisfactions of your job. What you have to say will be a great help to them in approaching the job market.

This is your ideal opportunity to find out not just the duties of a certain position, but how they are carried out, what business interactions occur, what a typical working day may look like, the excitement versus the routine, and the skills needed to perform well. This type of setting allows you to ask questions you could not ask in a job interview. Go after these important pieces of information and be prepared to ask your questions intelligently. Good preparation and follow-up on your part will greatly increase the value of these meetings to you.

BEFORE THE INTERVIEW:

- Make sure you are in business dress, which is appropriate for these interviews.
- Do your self-analysis. This will promote a more effective interchange and give you a better idea of how you would function in the area you are exploring.
- Research the company and industry. This will allow you to skip the basics and learn some of the finer points during the meeting.
- Determine and organize in your mind what you want to find out. This will help you to keep the conversation going whenever the ball is in your court.

AFTER THE INTERVIEW:

- Remember to write a letter of thanks to the person you visited.
- Take good notes on your meeting. They will be useful in the future.

Here in a nutshell are suggestions from the Columbia Business School Library as to the most popular places to look for information about a company in preparation for an interview. Use one or all depending on the amount of time you can spare and the seriousness of the interview. Remember that the company's *annual report* is always an excellent starting point too, but, while it is *about* the company, it is also *by* the company and therefore needs to be rounded out and rendered objective by other sources. Since it comes out only once a year, it also needs to be updated. The sources described below feature very current information and will put you light years ahead of someone who relies only on the annual report to find out what's happening in the company.

The *Value Line Investment Survey* offers the biggest return for the smallest investment in time. In ten minutes the *Value Line* will give you on one page more useful, current information about a company's products and prospects than anywhere else. Each company is reviewed quarterly and certain important figures are updated weekly.

Value Line does not cover all public companies, however, so if you need data on a smaller or less well known public company try the Standard & Poor's New York Stock Exchange Stock Reports, also known as the "tear-sheets," which reviews all New York and American Stock Exchange and most over-the-counter companies also on a quarterly basis.

For an investment of another fifteen minutes, the *F & S Index of Corporations and Industries* will show you all the recent articles about a company in the major trade, business, and financial periodicals such as *Fortune, Forbes, The Wall Street Journal, The New York Times, Advertising Age, Oil and Gas Journal, Electronic News,* and others. You can either go to the journals themselves and read the articles (date and page numbers are given), read only the *major* articles marked with a dot "o," or simply read all the one-line abstracts in the recent issues of the index, which comes out weekly. These summaries alone will give you a good picture of the newsworthy goings-on at the company and will help you find that juicy feature story that you suspect exists.

For callbacks and *very* serious interviews, we recommend a *computerized* literature search which, while requiring a modest investment of capital, will pay large dividends in terms of the time you will save and the thoroughness of your knowledge of the company. The business school library will search *Predicasts* and Dow Jones data bases and deliver to you a computer printout of references and abstracts of very current articles. Such a search can be especially valuable in finding specialized information or information on private companies such as most investment banks, advertising agencies, or management consulting firms. It rounds up most of the recent news about a company for you and saves you the trouble. Plan ahead.

The following will help you to find information about companies.

Directories (General)

There are a variety of company directories. Some are general lists of larger companies; others are specialized, either by location (country, state, or city) or by industry or trade. Some give fairly extensive information while others give address or industry only.

Standard & Poor's Register of Corporations, Directors & Executives. Alphabetical list of approximately thirty-seven thousand U.S. and Canadian corporations, giving officers, products (if manufacturer), standard industrial classification (SIC), sales range, and number of employees. Volume 2 consists of brief information on about seventy-five thousand executives and directors. An index of companies by SIC number as well as a geographical index is in Volume 3.

Million Dollar Directory. Dun & Bradstreet. 3 volumes. Lists approximately 120,000 large, medium, and small U.S. companies in volumes 1, 2, and 3, respectively. Gives officers, products (if manufacturer), standard industrial classification, approximate sales, and number of employees. The yellow pages list companies geographically and the blue pages by SIC number.

If the company is a manufacturer, you may find it listed in the following comprehensive directory:

Thomas Register of American Manufacturers. 16 volumes, annual. Volumes 1–8 list manufacturers by specific product. Volumes 9–10 are an alphabetical list of companies and include addresses, branch offices, brand names, subsidiaries, products, and estimated capitalization. Volumes 11–16 contain catalogs of products.

REGIONAL AND STATE INDUSTRIAL DIRECTORIES

If the industrial company is not in *Thomas* and you know in what area it is located, you may find it in a regional directory. For example:

California Manufacturers Register.
Directory of Central Atlantic States Manufacturers.
Directory of New England Manufacturers.
If it is a New York company, you might try:
New York State Industrial Directory.
Directory of Directors in the City of New York.

DIRECTORIES OF COMPANIES IN FOREIGN COUNTRIES

In the collection of directories of foreign companies, which emphasize western European countries and Canada, are the following:

Principal International Businesses (Dun & Bradstreet).
Canadian Trade Index.
Jane's Major Companies of Europe.
To find an industrial directory for a particular country, check the main library catalog under the country followed by "Industries—Directories," e.g., "Germany—Industries—Directories."

DIRECTORIES OF AMERICAN COMPANIES WITH FOREIGN SUBSIDIARIES

Directory of American Firms Operating in Foreign Countries.
Directory of Corporate Affiliations.

DIRECTORIES OF FOREIGN COMPANIES WITH AMERICAN SUBSIDIARIES

Directory of Foreign Firms Operating within the United States.
American Subsidiaries of German Firms.
Directory of Foreign Manufacturers in the United States.

DIRECTORIES OF SPECIFIC INDUSTRIES

If you are looking for a directory of companies within a specific industry or trade, check the main catalog under the industry followed by the subdivision directories, as "Textile Industry—Directories." A few examples:

Davison's Textile Blue Book.
Fairchild's Financial Manual of Retail Stores.
Electronic News Financial Fact Book and Directory.

DIRECTORIES OF NONMANUFACTURING OR SERVICE INDUSTRIES

Information on these firms is often more difficult to find than on those manufacturing a product. Often the industry is composed of many small, usually nonpublic companies—as in advertising, management consulting, or import-export industries. As with other industry directories, you should check the main catalog under the industry followed by "Directories," as "Business Consultants—Directories," or "Real Estate—U.S.—Directories." Some specific examples:

Standard Directory of Advertising Agencies.
American Register of Exporters & Importers.
International Directory of Marketing Research Houses and Services.
Consultants and Consulting Organizations Directory.
National Real Estate Investor Directory.

DIRECTORIES OF BANKING AND FINANCE

Most business libraries have many directories related to banking and finance. Among the areas represented are investment banking, insurance, mutual funds, and commercial banking. Some examples:

Polk's World Bank Directory.

The Corporate Finance Sourcebook. Karen Zehring. A directory of the financial community: investment bankers, commercial banks, U.S. based foreign banks, insurance lenders, etc.

Money Market Directory. A directory of six thousand institutional investors and their portfolio managers.

Best's Insurance Report: Life Health.

Best's Insurance Report: Property-Casualty.

INVESTMENT BANKING FIRMS

Finance: Investment Banker-Broker Directory.
Investment Dealers' Digest: Corporate Financing Directory.
Security Dealers of North America.

GUIDES TO DIRECTORIES AND OTHER SOURCES OF INFORMATION ON COMPANIES

If you have not found a directory for the specific industry or area you want, you might check a bibliography of directories that may list a trade directory your library does not have, or you may check a directory issue of a trade journal. Among the most comprehensive guides are:

Guide to American Directories.

European Companies: A Guide to Sources of Information. G. P. Henderson.

Encyclopedia of Business Information Sources.
Trade Directories of the World.

Articles About Companies

Predicasts F & S Index to Corporations and Industries: United States. Weekly, cumulates monthly, quarterly, and annually. Indexes articles on companies and industries that have appeared in a wide range of financial, trade, and business publications.

F & S Europe. Monthly, cumulates quarterly and annually. An index similar to the one above, for European companies.

F & S Index International. Monthly, cumulates quarterly and annually. An index similar to the ones above, for companies in other than the United States or Europe.

Wall Street Journal Index. Monthly, cumulates annually. Each issue has two parts: "Corporate News" and "General News." Indexing is based on the Eastern Edition final.

Wall Street Transcript. Weekly. A compilation of brokerage house reports on companies and industries. Each issue is indexed, and there is a periodic cumulation.

Financial Information About Companies

Financial information is generally available only for those companies which are publicly held. Most companies, though they may be corporations, are private and therefore not required to disclose financial information to the public. These include most advertising, import-export, consulting, accounting, and investment banking firms. Do not expect to find financial information on these companies.

For sources of financial information on public companies, NYSE, ASE, or OTC, see the checklist titled "Information Sources for Investment Analysis" at the library reference desk. Sources include Standard & Poor's and

Moody's manuals, investment surveys, brokerage house reports, and others.

Corporation Records

Most business school libraries collect the following documents for companies listed on the New York and American Stock Exchanges:

Annual Reports to Shareholders
Listing Statements
Proxy Statements
10-K Reports to the SEC

Histories of Companies

Some business school libraries have a collection of published histories of companies. These are ordinarily catalogued under the name of the company in the main library catalog.

INDEX